The Call of Trains

The Call of Trains

Railroad Photographs by Jim Shaughnessy

text by Jeff Brouws

W. W. Norton & Company   New York   London

Dedication

This book is dedicated to my wife, Carol, who for almost fifty years has been encouraging, tolerant, and proud of my accomplishments, as well as being a traveling companion on many expeditions to less than comfortable destinations.

Introduction

Of all the great
modern inventions,
the railroad is
possibly the one
to which American
artists have accorded
the most significance.

Leo Marx
*The Railroad in
American Art* [1]

Railroading Landscapes:
The Photographs of Jim Shaughnessy   Jeff Brouws

Figure 1

Engineer of
Canadian National
4–6–2 #5288 leans
out cab window,
Bromptonville,
Quebec,
1957

The New England railroad landscape Jim Shaughnessy found himself born into was not far removed from the early-twentieth-century version romanticized by Stewart Holbrook in his *Story of American Railroads*.[2] For Holbrook, trains of promise, mystery, majesty, and surprising beauty ran through the Hegan Woods of Vermont, comprising a system of transport representing all that was primeval and original. That the Northeast served as one nexus point from which America's nascent railroad network sprang is indisputable. The Delaware & Hudson tested the *Sturbridge Lion*, the first steam locomotive in America, in 1829, and throughout the 1830s and 1840s the region's railroads became an enthralling technology that writers wrote about, painters filled canvases with, and philosophers commented on. Social critics at the time were questioning and tentative, but most evinced excitement at the railroad's future prospects—and anxiously waited to see what, if any, transformative effect this harbinger of progress might have on culture and custom at the outset of America's industrial revolution.

Painters such as Asher Durand, George Inness, and others included steam locomotives and diminutive trains in their artwork, contextualizing them within the deep spaces of their compositions.[3] Transcendentalist writers like Henry David Thoreau[4] and Ralph Waldo Emerson[5] penned paragraphs, in positive and negative tone, about the railroad's impact on the environment and human agency. Clearly, the railroad's presence provoked much thought and became part of the visual culture of the times; its growing significance was recognized in broad intellectual, emotional, and aesthetic terms.

It's only natural, then, that a young photographer, living in upstate New York at mid-twentieth century, might inherit these strands of native curiosity generated by the region's proto-artists and scholars— a curiosity that brought him trackside to record his own discoveries and impressions. When Jim Shaughnessy walked downtown to Troy's train station for the first time in the winter of 1945, little did he realize that he would become the creator of a vast archive focused primarily on New England railroading and its final engagement with the age of steam. Fortuitously, the resonant whistles of Delaware & Hudson's elephant-eared 4–8–4 Northerns aroused his interest and charmed his imagination. They called and he responded.

Shaughnessy and His Environment:
Foreground / Background

Located 150 miles from New York City, Troy is nestled at the confluence of two rivers and two canals—the Mohawk and Hudson, Erie and Champlain respectively. In 1786 the village of Van der Heyden came into being out of an existing land grant, and three years later changed its name to Troy.[6] The location of this early Dutch settlement was chosen wisely; an important trading center developed, following the arc of the eighteenth century's industrial revolution. In the nineteenth century, continuing its upward progression, Troy morphed into a signature industrial city of the Northeast. It became an overnight sensation with the invention of detachable shirt collars and cuffs in 1827.[7]

By the 1860s, heavy industry got into the act, as four of the country's largest mills and foundries called Troy home. The belching smokestacks of the Rensselaer Iron Works, the Clinton Iron Foundry, the Bessemer Steel Works, and the Albany Iron Works (which rolled the iron plates used on the Union's ironclad ship *Monitor*)[8] signaled prosperity, and products essential to a rapidly expanding nation—horseshoes, rail spikes, stoves, bells, nails, and wheels—rolled away from their loading docks. Commerce was solid for half a century; factories blossomed everywhere. In 1910 alone, the city claimed to have 612 production facilities.[9] After the Armistice of 1918 and the end of the Great War, the good times began trending away. An economic shift, begun at the turn of the century as manufacturing concerns relocated to the Midwest, was now definitely in the air.[10]

Jim Shaughnessy was born into this twentieth-century environment on November 24, 1933, just as the area's industrial base began to erode. The railroads that he would later know well were entering a transitional period that would have lasting effects. The New York Central, Boston & Maine, Rutland, and Delaware & Hudson still ran, not yet close to collapse, but the clock was ticking for both the city and its transportation systems. A great "rearranging of everyone's life" was occurring.[11] America was at the height of the Depression, 13 million people were out of work across the country,[12] and President Roosevelt had been elected to office twelve months earlier.

Jim's parents, Helen Goodwin and James A. Shaughnessy, had been married four years earlier, just months prior to the crash of 1929. His mother worked as a secretary for the W. & L. E. Gurley Company, a firm specializing in surveying instruments and esoteric measuring devices.[13] Jim's father worked at Saint Joseph's Seminary as the superintendent of buildings and grounds, a job he'd taken in the mid-1920s in an effort to secure more stable employment. Previously he had followed his own father's footsteps into the mechanical trades and worked as a machinist at Tolhars Machine Shop, near the train station downtown.

The seminary—a Romanesque building poised on the eastern crest of the Hudson Valley, overlooking the city of Troy and adjacent to Rensselaer Polytechnic Institute—had a fabled history with various owners and Orders.[14] The Shaughnessy family lived in a small house on the grounds. Jim's father's duties included attending to the boiler room and steam plant (later converted to diesel) that provided electricity to the facility. Young Jim helped his father work on this equipment, often disassembling it, cleaning it, and putting it back together. The mechanics involved were fascinating. This early exposure to machinery is where his interest in steam locomotion began; perhaps a broader appreciation for the industrial (or technological) sublime was also a by-product. This work, along with lawn mowing, snow plowing, raking leaves, and similar odd jobs, gave Jim enjoyment, as he liked the solitude that working around the seminary grounds afforded him, preferring solo activities to "shooting baskets" with the other boys.[15] These chores provided him with necessary pocket change, supplying the financial means to fund his first passion: rail photography. For a while, too, between the ages of seven and nine, he also played classical piano, but it didn't take; the trains, it seems, trumped his other interests.

A "favorite and understanding" uncle, Cornelius Shaughnessy, became a pivotal influence on the young Shaughnessy's growing interest in railroading.[16] "Con," a former valve setter on Delaware & Hudson steam locomotives at its Colonie shops (a job he held for about five years during the 1920s), later became a boiler inspector for the Hartford Insurance Company and would occasionally take Jim along when he conducted inspections. On their rounds they stopped by railroad locations like engine facilities, with the uncle explaining crossheads, cylinders, or valve gear to Jim. They both enjoyed seeing the locomotives and discussing their attributes, and they bonded around this activity.[17]

Jim had come from a lineage of mechanically inclined men—a key factor when considering his lifelong infatuation with trains and the career in civil engineering he would later pursue. His grandfather, also named James, and originally born with the surname of O'Shaughnessy

in Kildimo, County Limerick, Ireland, in 1861, worked at the West Virginia Pulp and Paper mill in Mechanicville, New York, as a mechanic. O'Shaughnessy, whose own family had survived Ireland's potato famine in the 1840s, decided to immigrate to America in the early 1880s by himself, seeking greater economic opportunity. He became one of many who entered the U.S. during the second great wave of European immigration, providing cheap labor for an industrializing, expanding nation.[18] While many immigrants settled where their ships landed, Jim's grandfather took an additional step, making the voyage up the Hudson River to Mechanicville, ten miles north of Troy. Those of Irish descent constituted almost 50 percent of the area's population in the 1880s, providing a degree of familiarity to a foreigner on new soil. The elder O'Shaughnessy's decision to emigrate from Ireland, settle in the area, and raise a family would prove propitious for the historic development of railfan photography in America for two reasons: first, his grandson would help to define a new visual paradigm for photographing American trains and railroads seventy-five years later; and second, Mechanicville would become a base camp and crossroads—an observation post, really—from which Shaughnessy the adult would record the evolution and contraction of Northeastern railroading in the latter half of the twentieth century.

When young Shaughnessy descended into the bustling, boisterous avenues of downtown Troy to make train pictures for the first time—this in 1946, at age thirteen—he had no underlying intention or motivation to undo or surpass what had already been done pictorially. At this point railroad photography was for him neither art nor mere documentation, but a set of intuitive choices and possibilities, which he allowed himself free rein to explore. His curiosity fanned the flames of a growing interest in things mechanical (trains), and, by using a piece of technology (a camera), coupling it to the sciences of light and chemical reaction (photography), he was able to record what he saw. This alchemy, later carried into the darkroom, delighted him. Beyond the science and physics of camerawork, however, what did the urban landscape, the trains traversing it, and the interrelationships between the two, aesthetically or intellectually, disclose to Jim as he began to interact with them photographically?

Right below the seminary, perched on the top step of the Approach (a staircase erected in 1907 to provide easy access between Rensselaer Polytechnic Institute and downtown)—and no more than a half mile from the front steps of the cottage where the family resided—Shaughnessy could view Troy's diverse cityscape from on high. Here, over snow-covered rooftops (see fig. 2), he spied train movements down on Broadway and in between the closely marshaled buildings of the central business district—topography very typical of the

Figures 3, 4, 5, and 6, clockwise:

Shaughnessy's darkroom, circa 1949; Early photograph made at Castleton-on-Hudson, New York, processed at Knowlson's drugstore, 1945; shot made from locomotive cab of NYC 4–6–4 Hudson #5272 and local train along "Collar City's" Metropolitan Corridor, 1946; Tower #1 and the *Laurentian*, 1951. All other images from Troy, New York.

urbanized Northeast. Steaming tugboats hauling coal barges or the occasional pleasure boat (one of which his father owned) on the Hudson would have caught his eye. He would have noticed, too, the rumbling cadence of the numerous passenger trains that plied the city streets, making stops beneath Union Station's canopied platforms.

Once off the Approach's cut-granite steps, and alighting on Broadway, he might greet friends who were signal maintainers working around the depot, or ascend the stairs of Tower 1 to get a lineup (a list of trains coming into or through the station area) and have a chat with the operator. This particular interlocking plant, guarding train movements into the depot, straddled the north-south mainlines in a unique, utilitarian fashion, because the downtown's commercial and residential districts—not to mention numerous vehicular crossings—pressed so tightly in against the railroad right-of-way. This structure figured in several early Shaughnessy images (see fig. 6) and was perhaps the most intriguing architectural feature he encountered in Troy's railroad landscape and its quintessential "Metropolitan Corridor," a term coined by cultural geographer John Stilgoe, who has written so eloquently about this facet of the American viewscape (see fig. 7).[19]

In the late 1940s Delaware & Hudson 4–8–4 Northerns with the *Laurentian* in tow, or New York Central's ubiquitous 4–6–4 Hudsons, could be seen steaming along Sixth Avenue, cylinder cocks open, their full-throated whistles occasionally calling out; a decade later the dieselized chant of maroon and gold Boston & Maine E7s would join, and then supplant, that chorus. A constellation of elements found within the rail environment—sounds, smells, the compelling mechanics and aesthetics of steam and diesel technologies—created an internal fascination for young Shaughnessy. It was here that Jim received his baptism into the world of railroading, and over the next sixty years, using a variety of cameras—from Rolleis to Nikons, Kodak Bullets to Speed Graphics—he systematically documented and covered all the trains and territory his time and energy allowed.

Influences, Frames of Reference

Jim attended Catholic school, first the St. Francis de Sales grade school, and then Catholic Central High, parochial education being the norm for Irish and Italian families at this time. He also took part in church services. In high school Reverend Raymond Halpin, who managed yearbook preparation and gave casual instruction in photography, befriended him. Jim received lessons from Halpin on rudimentary photographic technique and darkroom processes. A former student of Halpin's named Leo Bouchard, who freelanced around Troy doing weddings and other commercial work, also passed along technical expertise to Shaughnessy at this formative stage.

Jim recalls Halpin speaking about Canadian photographer Yosuf Karsh's dramatic portraiture, which Jim had seen.[20] It is interesting to speculate on two points when considering the nighttime locomotive portraits that became part of Shaughnessy's signature style. Did "Karsh of Ottawa's" use of strong light, creating dramatic contrast with deep shadows, inspire Jim's use of similar tonalities when he began taking more risks with flash photography after 1951? Did the concept of taking a studio "portrait" (and controlling all aspects of lighting) come to Shaughnessy after seeing Karsh's photography too, eager as he was to make dramatic, unconventional images of locomotives (see fig. 26)?

Working on the school's yearbook from 1948–51, Jim made his first prints in Halpin's at-home darkroom. These were for school publications and not images of trains, despite the fact that he was, at this point, already thoroughly engaged with the hobby of railroad photography. The earliest known train pictures Shaughnessy made were exposed around Troy's Union Station in 1945–46. They were processed and printed at Knowlson's, a local drugstore that had a photo department where Jim bought one of his first cameras, a Kodak 35.[21] The diminutive, deckle-edged contact prints made by Knowlson's were recently unearthed in the Shaughnessy files and live in the world as multidimensional artifacts. They're evidence of a budding photographic talent, they reference a specific time and place in railroad history, and they are mementos of a bygone era when drugstores were the principal purveyors of the nation's snapshots (see fig. 4). Some of these images were made into larger prints after Jim and his father built a home darkroom in 1949 (see fig. 3).

In 1948, seminal events occurred for Shaughnessy, and important friendships were forged. He met fellow traveler and railfan Sandy Worthen on a Capital District Railroad Club trip on the Fonda, Johnstown & Gloversville Railroad. Worthen, a resident of Montreal who was a chemist by profession and a founding member of the Canadian Railway Historical Association, played a key role in shaping Jim's future aesthetic and attitude toward what he photographed along the high iron. He introduced Jim to the geography and landscapes of Canada's Eastern Townships, sharing knowledge of an unfamiliar culture while providing novel insights into the railroad history and engineering works found in La Belle Province. Worthen, according to rail photographer Greg McDonnell, "had a broad conceptual appreciation for history, as well as a refined understanding of a 'sense of place.' "[22] He saw the interrelationships between sociology, technology, economics, history, and geography found within the man-made and natural landscapes of the railroading world he witnessed and studied—and "of course" the twin bands of steel "blended and focused all these interests."[23] Talkative and didactic, Worthen

Figure 7
New York Central *Laurentian,* and observation car, Troy Union Station, Troy, New York, 1958

enjoyed lively discussion and sharing knowledge. On a practical level, being bilingual in Canada helped immensely in gaining access to locomotive facilities and yards: Shaughnessy researched the locations, and Worthen, using his contacts and fluent French, "talked" them in, securing vital information on train movements. Shaughnessy's Canadian National and Canadian Pacific images are among the strongest photographs in his archive. This suggests that Worthen's friendship, affection for rural environments (which Jim shared), intellectual rigor, observational skills, and the happy camaraderie between the two while railfanning together had a profound, sparking influence on Shaughnessy's creative development.

Their intellectual compatibility was a plus too; they conversed on a wide range of topics, from the Revolutionary War to Renaissance music, and seemed quite at ease in each other's company. Sandy would come out east from Montreal, meeting Jim at his parents' home in Ayres Cliff, Quebec, where they stayed when traveling in the area. The pair collaborated on several articles for *Trains* magazine, one on Mount Washington's cog railway in July 1956, the other on the Quebec bridge over the St. Lawrence River in March 1985, with Sandy handling the verbiage and Jim the visuals, utilizing either his own photography or historic images from his archive. Shaughnessy counts Worthen, along with John Pickett, as the traveling companions he had the deepest connections to—for Jim, the enjoyment and companionship of these trips transcended pressing the camera's shutter button.[24]

In October 1948 the Exchange Club of Chatham began sponsoring 1890s-themed steam runs on the Rutland Railway's Chatham Branch to Manchester, Vermont (see fig. 8). In the years between 1949 and 1951 Curt Law went with Jim. He was a fellow student and friend who was also a member of the Rensselaer Model Railroad Society at RPI, a club Jim got involved with around the same time (and would be an active member of for fifteen years). In the first year of this excursion, as Shaughnessy and Law photographed the high-stepping Alco ten-wheeler #77 at rest in Manchester—and with the engine crew about to make a shuttle run to Rutland before returning to Chatham—engineer Raymond Hazeltine asked the teenagers, cameras dangling around their necks, whether they'd like a cab ride. They jumped at the chance; this was the first of several cab-riding experiences in which Shaughnessy would find himself the lucky participant over the next thirty years (see Rutland Railroad Historic Society's *Newsliner,* Spring 2001, pp. 4–8 and *Magnetic North*, Boston Mills Publications, 1999, p. 60). With the retirement of the Rutland's wooden coaches the Chatham Branch was abandoned in 1953, effectively eliminating passenger service on the line. The excursions ended but the friendships did not. The camaraderie fashioned by these trips with Worthen and Law was

long-lasting and life-altering, and provided Jim with a support network for his railfanning activities. John Pickett was on the last run but wouldn't meet Jim until 1954, while both were visiting at Phil Hastings's home in Selkirk, New York—a visit portentously placing Shaughnessy and Hastings into each other's creative orbits for several years—perhaps a key development in the history of American railroad photography when one compares the two photographers' complimentary styles.

In this early period, between 1946 and 1951, Shaughnessy's mother and father were very accommodating of their son's growing interest in railroading, taking him on day trips and weekend jaunts (monthly occurrences that lasted throughout the 1950s). These Sunday drives, which were a common social event in post–World War II America after years of gas rationing and truncated car trips, were delightful, relaxed tours of the New England countryside. The Shaughnessy family enjoyed getting out into the unsullied Northeastern landscapes. The 1949 two-toned gray Chevy owned by Jim's father was often found in the Cadosia station parking lot on the New York, Ontario & Western line or tooling along two-lane roads, up the Champlain Valley to destinations in rural Vermont or upstate New York on the Rutland or Delaware & Hudson railroads.

The first stop when pulling into a new town was the local depot. Jim and his father would engage the operator (one worked at every country depot) about train movement information, supplementing the already encyclopedic knowledge Jim was acquiring from magazines and official guides. While the father shared his son's interest in railroading, he took no photographs, content to just look and be a part of the experience. Jim's mother, along for the ride, sat in the car and usually read. With steam still in service, Shaughnessy remembers, "there were a lot of great trains running" so they never lacked for things to see. He also recalls that something as simple as a place-name could arouse familial enthusiasm. "Rutland was such an evocative name for a railroad and town, and that's how I got started with that company . . .we all just had to go there and check it out."

Looking back, this phase of Jim's youth occurred during "the final swan song for much that he found intriguing":[25] it was also a ground zero point for his developing talent. By this time, with a Kodak Bullet 127 camera (which cost $2.75 and made eight frames per roll on 127 film that were $1^{5}/_{8}''$ x $2^{1}/_{2}''$ in size),[26] he shot with passion, and it wasn't just about the locomotives. He encouraged his parents to participate in the process too. This decision to place passengers, parents, or workers within the context of the railroad landscape, adjacent to buildings or equipment, became an important component of his emerging style. By seeing the railroad milieu as social space, he humanized the industrial environment, exploring the relationships between the railroad and the people that interacted with it.

Figure 8

Exchange Club Special with Jim Shaughnessy (second from left) and Curt Law (far right). Rutland, Vermont, 1949

The Milwaukee School Writ Large

During this late adolescent phase, Shaughnessy also began making distinctions between urban and rural environments, ruminating on what kind of location he liked for train photography; he grew to favor the "bucolic over the built-up."[27] He may have also unconsciously begun to think about the type or style of photography he wanted to do.

One of his very early heroes, outside the railfan photographic fraternity, was Ansel Adams; Shaughnessy, in fact, made nature images (mountaintops and clouds) in the Adams mode (with a newly acquired 4 x 5) at Rocky Mountain National Park while on a trip to Colorado in 1951 with Father Halpin. Jim notes that, except for Adams, he wasn't familiar with other contemporaneous American photographers, such as Walker Evans, Jack Delano, John Vachon, Robert Frank, or W. Eugene Smith,[28] a fact that brings into question the lineage of influence affecting mid-century American railroad photography, at least as it pertains to Shaughnessy and perhaps many of his railfan contemporaries. It will be recalled that Evans eschewed scenic landscape images[29] preferring instead to photograph vernacular architecture in urban and small-town environments where the "hand of man" dominated (Delano and Vachon were attracted to similar objects). Clearly, these three artists, based on their preferences in subject matter, would not have been a direct influence on Shaughnessy, with his predilection for the pastoral view, even if he had known about them. Evans and his Farm Security Administration cohorts were unfamiliar names in mainstream America (except to a select cadre of photography world insiders). While Evans's "American Photographs" show at the Museum of Modern Art in 1938 garnered some attention at the time, it wasn't until FSA images appeared at another MoMA exhibition in 1962—"The Bitter Years: 1935–41," curated by Edward Steichen[30]—that people in the general population and larger art world began to take notice of these important photographers. The burgeoning fine-art photography market in the United States brought their work to wider audiences in the mid-1970s and early 1980s. While a smattering of FSA work (often not credited) found its way into the popular press and photography magazines like *Look* and *US Camera Annual* in the 1930s and 1940s, it's almost impossible to gauge its effect on railfan photographers shooting during the same era.[31] Shaughnessy, though not a subscriber to photography periodicals, recalls seeing Dust Bowl images in *Life*.[32] Several images by Russell Lee (another FSA photographer) of the Rio Grande Southern narrow-gauge appeared in the February 1942 issue of *Trains*, but they don't stand out as something to imitate—they blend aesthetically with the rest of the issue's content.[33] Jack Delano's documentary project on American railroading, completed in 1943

while working for the Office of War Information, didn't appear in a form readily recognizable or accessible to the railfan audience until the late 1970s, when James E. Valle published a broad selection (292 images) in *The Iron Horse at War* (Howell-North Books, 1977). So it's a curiosity and a point to ponder: did these FSA photographers, who are extremely well known to us *now* in 2008, actually have an impact on those railfan photographers in the late 1930s, 1940s, and 1950s, who seemed uninterested in American or European photography trends outside the realm of railfan picture making? It seems not. (Informally questioning railfan photographers young and old, I've found few interested in the deeper history of photography).

I would assert a similar lack of influence for the work of Robert Frank or Gene Smith on Shaughnessy's photography. Frank, employing small 35mm Leicas, used a fluid snapshot aesthetic in his compositions. Characterized by somber tones, grainy moodiness, and off-kilter framing, the pictures suggest a foreboding alienation afoot in America.[34] This interpretive style of photography wasn't what Jim practiced; the content of Jim's images was rendered in a factual, unemotional way, with no sociopolitical or aesthetic agenda. He was taking photographs of subjects he felt an affinity for, not distance from. Smith operated in a very measured photo-story mode, dependent upon groupings of pictures to carry a dramatic, human-based, or socially relevant narrative (usually focused on one individual or theme, such as Albert Schweitzer or the city of Pittsburgh).[35] Jim's approach was more casual and not configured around a storyboard or layout. The pictures comprising his articles appearing in *Trains* were for the most part assembled after the fact, and were generalized representations of whatever railroad was before his lens, usually oriented toward equipment. His photography was based more on a documentary approach than a storytelling one.

Shaughnessy's archive bears these differentiations out: there are thousands of images of trains in pastoral landscapes, and only a handful of urban railroad scenes. Railroad architecture isn't a front-and-center concern of his (like it was for Evans or David Plowden), nor is there an overt emphasis on the human condition (as in the work of Frank and Smith), or a desire to capture the instantaneous, "decisive moment" (like Henri Cartier-Bresson) versus the appreciation of a prolonged gaze that Shaughnessy's photography affords us.

Also, unlike Richard Steinheimer or Ted Benson later—train photographers who consciously conceptualized photo-based stories for publication about specific railroaders, railroads, or places *before* taking the pictures—Jim's notoriety stems more from the multitude of well-known single images (see pls. 6, 81, and 89) that span his sixty-year career. When his photography accompanied an article in *Trains* (he was a favorite of editor David P. Morgan for the frontispiece motif), it usually ran as supportive illustration for the text, with the words and pictures forming a balanced mix, not as a photo essay driven by the imagery—a subtle but important distinction. Naturally, there are a few exceptions—an article on the Baltimore & Ohio's Lake Branch in the January 1956 issue, and another on the Chicago, Burlington & Quincy's O-5 locomotive from May 1957 come to mind. However, in the main, the approaches outlined above leave little doubt as to what kind of geography, subject matter, and photographic style he favored.

So if he wasn't influenced directly by the most important practitioners of mainstream American photography in the fifties, from where did his inspiration spring? Looking at Shaughnessy's work, and ticking down the list of photographers he admired and found influential (James LaVake, William Pontin, Richard Steinheimer, Robert Hale, Philip Hastings, H. Reid, J. Parker Lamb, William Middleton, and O. Winston Link),[36] the evidence suggests that his biggest source of visual inspiration bloomed from within the pages of *Trains* magazine. These lensmen, along with underappreciated staff photographers from the same publication such as Wally Abbey, W. A. Akin, Willard V. Anderson, A. C. Kalmbach, and Linn Wescott together formed what I've come to call the Milwaukee School. These were the artists truly pushing the hobby in new directions, helping to redefine the aesthetics of train photography during this era, through word and picture. Abbey, Akin, and Steinheimer had extensive backgrounds in journalism and photojournalism;[37] Hale graduated from Art Center in Pasadena; Hastings and Reid were autodidacts who relied on their own internal muses (as did Shaughnessy); Link brought an engineering background and brilliant commercial photographic technique—with elaborate film noir lighting and staging effects—to bear on his nocturnal Norfolk & Western imagery.[38]

Railfan lensmen during this era (and authors like Lucius Beebe and editors like Morgan) also sensed intuitively that photographs might be multilayered and "read" in different ways. Pictures could act as simple documents giving an accurate record of the object before the camera, and also function as vehicles for social commentary, be narrative in nature or aesthetically inclined, containing graphic details relying on formalism or notions of beauty. They might be stand-alone masterpieces or a suite of images coupled to a supporting text relating a compelling story.

There were also other philosophical and intellectual shifts occurring in the field: Morgan as editor ran interesting articles that hinted at a broader cultural awareness of railroads and railroading, contextualizing how they meshed with American life, as seen in the September 1953 issue,[39] which used full-page photography to illustrate his theme. Under his tutelage, his charges were pressed to see it all in a new way, with several articles appearing during the 1950s that spoke specifically about railroad photography and showcased veteran and young Turk cameramen (including Shaughnessy) doing the best, most inventive work in the field.[40]

These perceptive insights were novel when considered within the context of photographs made by the majority of railfans in the late 1940s, which generally were concerned with straight documentation, a faithful rendering of what lay before the camera. Taken in a direct manner, these images were nonartistic. In this group, there was minimal experimentation or exploration of the properties inherent in the mechanics, physics, and aesthetics of photography itself.

Few photographers toyed with shutter speeds and optics, or thought about the effects of light and temporality, or explored the significance of shapes, shadows, or contrasts within their compositions; photography was a means to an end, not an end in itself. Jim Shaughnessy, however, and a small crew of his colleagues (Hale, Steinheimer, and Hastings, among others), did do these things and started thinking more *photographically*. Collectively, they broke through the calcified bedrock of the three-quarter wedge-shot tradition with curiosity and creativity, developing a new visual language for railroad photography that found its way, slowly but surely, into the railfan print media throughout the 1950s, 1960s, and 1970s. Because of these innovations, railroad pictures were lifted into the realm of art for the first time, warranting a different consideration. Forty years later, by the fiftieth anniversary issue of *Trains* in November 1990, no one doubted that images of trains could be artful. That issue reveled in the positive photographic achievements of the hobby. Later *Trains* editors Kevin Keefe, Mark Hemphill, and Jim Wrinn added their own sensibilities to the mix, further defining what constituted interesting railroad photography through their brave editorial selections.

As part of this advance guard in the 1950s, Shaughnessy et al. made conscious decisions to see beyond the trains, embracing the "ugly beauty" of industrial environments too.[41] This was a profound decision. Most amateur photographers of the day did "calendar photography," snapshots of "scenics," sunsets, or pictures of a favorite pet, family activity, or car. Rarely, if ever, did they venture into gritty and dangerous industrial zones. A railfan photographer would have been thought an odd duck for photographing "dirty" locomotives. Despite this outsider status, these photographers forged ahead, relying on intuition and passion. They buoyed themselves (and their craft) with a healthy dose of self-reliance coupled to an inner drive that bordered on, and even crossed over into, obsession. As Shaughnessy's various aesthetic choices demonstrate—the desire to include the human element, the desire to place the trains and locomotives in broader contextual spaces, or the desire to explore the railroad after dark[42]—the man from Troy was a germinating

force within this school of American train photography taking root in the late 1940s and early 1950s.

After graduating from twelfth grade in June 1951, Jim had an insufficient math background to matriculate to RPI, so he went north to Champlain College in Plattsburgh, New York, to gain the necessary credits. A rustic educational setting located just south of the Canadian border, the college was a converted army barracks and military staging area used during World War I. Shaughnessy's dorm room in Saratoga Hall overlooked the D&H mainline and a long passing siding needed for train operations,[43] giving him a bird's-eye view of the traffic flowing on the railroad. One evening, symbol-freight RW-2 (the overnight

paper train that ran from Rouses Point, New York, to Wilkes-Barre, Pennsylvania) set out a cut of cars. In Shaughnessy's description (quoting Lucius Beebe), "it looked like the burning of Rome" when the engineer got his train rolling again on the slight southbound grade out of town. Jim recalls the concussive beat of the steam exhaust, the rattling of his dorm windows: experiences not to be forgotten. Such exhilarating pyrotechnical displays of routine railroading, and a young student's lucky proximity to them, left indelible impressions, igniting creative impulses that he later succeeded in getting onto film (see fig. 9). With a newly purchased 4 x 5 Speed Graphic in hand (serial number 827493, a set of digits he remembers fifty-seven years later), he set about catching steam-powered locals, through freights, and passenger trains such as the *Laurentian* and *Montreal Limited* piloted by Pacifics, 4–8–4s, or the then newly minted Alco RS3 roadswitchers (dieselization began in 1951 on the D&H).

These events proved to be welcoming distractions from his studies and opened him to further pictorial and social possibilities. Being somewhat of a loner at this age, and away from home for the first time, Shaughnessy gravitated toward the local D&H depot for after-class and weekend camaraderie, forming a genial relationship with the station agent there. His Sunday routine was to take the mile walk into town, attend church, and make a weekly phone call to his parents from the bus station. Then, with religious and familial responsibilities taken care of, he'd while away the remaining hours of the afternoon at the depot.[44] Hanging around on the station platform or in the waiting room represented his continuing flirtation with the Delaware & Hudson—a railroad he established close ties with in 1945, which he would maintain over the next forty years.

Other things took place at school. A fellow engineering student and dormitory mate named Ronald Maumary, one in a long line of good-natured travel buddies, befriended him (and would transfer with Jim to RPI a year later). Maumary, not a railfan but a confirmed joyrider, had a 1941 Chevrolet. He delighted in driving Jim (during their RPI phase) into the surrounding countryside for what he termed "the three-state trip"— forays that included stops in Bennington, Vermont, to shoot the Rutland; Williamstown, Massachusetts, for the Boston & Maine, and then back home to Troy, New York, where they might encounter additional rail action, all in a four- to five-hour period.

While chasing trains usually involved one of these day jaunts, they'd occasionally stay overnight (on longer trips across the Green Mountain State and into New Hampshire), renting a two-dollar room in a guest home and cooking hot dogs over a campfire in a local park. At other times, and closer to campus (during their Plattsburgh sojourn), the two watched diesel-powered ferries tramp across Lake Champlain from Plattsburgh, fostering Jim's additional interest in water navigation

Figure 9

Delaware & Hudson
4–8–4 Northern #301
and freight train,
Plattsburgh, New York,
1952

and boats. Such inexpensive adventure was commonplace in small-town America in 1951; the two college students on slim budgets were only too happy to take advantage of it.[45]

While Shaughnessy engaged in intermittent rail photography at Champlain College, work in the darkroom had to wait. With no access to processing facilities on campus, his exposed film remained stashed away in light-tight Kodak boxes until Thanksgiving, Christmas, or Easter holidays brought him home to his parents' house in Troy, where he could dust off the enlarger, set up developing trays, mix chemicals, soup film, and make prints.

Later, in June 1955, after both graduated from RPI, Shaughnessy and Maumary took a celebratory road trip to California, ostensibly to drop Ron off at a new engineering job in Southern California. Never wandering far from transcontinental mainlines en route (the truer mission), Jim shot Southern Pacific F7s at Hazen, Nevada, and Union Pacific cab units at the station in Pomona, California, making a few record shots prior to boarding the *El Capitan* for his return trip home.

Time Books, Trips, and Friendships

Within three leather-bound "timekeeping" books Jim lent me for research purposes are the records of 132 trips made pursuing trains from 1954 through 1968 (at least the ones he wrote down). Not included are the monthly "Sunday drives" he took with his parents outlined above, or the quick thirty-minute treks to nearby locations like the Cohoes Bridge or Mechanicville yards. Detailed expense accounts for meals, motels, gas, phone calls, and other travel costs are listed faithfully. The tabulations also cite amounts received in payment for photos used by *Trains* or *Railway Age* for each trip taken, as sort of a way to keep track of "the money going out and coming in."

Above the trip entries, at the top of the page, he refers to the Montreal "run," Norfolk & Western "steam safari," or this "round-up," that "wrap-up," "caper," or "tour." The books' covers are a patinated caramel color and contain a calligraphic moderne typeface straight from the 1930s. "J SHAUGHNESSY, C.E." (civil engineer) appears in his own hand, etched with indelible ink at the lower edge of the booklet. The journals have the gravitas of Moses' tablets; I handle them respectfully (see fig. 12).

Though Jim recorded only mileage and expenses, the books' contents still provide a valuable, if bare bones, account of the seminal trips where so much of the photography occurred that established his growing reputation. Unfortunately, no expositional prose telegraphing impressions, feelings, snippets of conversation, or fragments of thought appears—but this is understandable: with all the train photography, when would he have had time to write too?

We do learn of the people he journeyed with, and from the place-names listed we can imagine provinces, townships, rivers, the lakes and landscapes he found himself in. We can place him in time and space with pinpoint precision and get a glimmer of the intensity with which he and his fellow photographers practiced railroad photography. Great distances were traversed quickly, with no superfluous activity mentioned—sightseeing was definitely not on the schedule. Chasing trains was the sole raison d'être for the trips, with steam the main item captivating their attention. While occasional family vacations with his mother and father, and later with his wife, Carol, insert themselves into this narrative of names and numbers, those trips are the exception rather than the rule. Shaughnessy rarely traveled alone on these junkets, preferring the friendship and company of fellow railfans.

Without a doubt, a certain brand of high-voltage youthful energy and enthusiasm fueled these expeditions. The treks were made during every season, in all kinds of weather, whether it was the hothouse humidity of a Painesville, Ohio, summer afternoon stalking double-headed, articulated 2–8–8–4 Yellowstones on the B&O's Lake Branch, or the cold-steely frostiness of a New England winter cab ride on the CN's *Bootlegger* (see *Classic Trains*, Winter 2005, pp. 40–45). Being impervious to harsh conditions was an essential: Jim tells the story of being in Vermont one time on the Saint Johnsbury & Lamiolle County, with temperatures at ten degrees below zero, and having his cheek freeze to the metal back of his 4 x 5 Speed Graphic. In another instance (in Montreal), a film pack shattered due to extreme cold, spraying pieces of celluloid everywhere. Despite these hardships and mishaps, comfort and caution were not priorities; the importance of the photographic hunt and what might lie ahead outweighed the bodily considerations of nourishment, sleep, or personal safety.

Names of numerous travel companions appear in capital letters: he made eight trips with Phil Hastings (Phil's son Steven also accompanied them several times), and he also traveled with Dick Adamson, Richard Baldwin, Bill Blakeman, Ken Chivers, Rod Craib, Raymond Halpin, Warren Hils, G. Johnson, John Krause, Curt Law, Ron Maumary, John Pickett, R. Ritchie, John Sliter, Craig Woodworth, and Sandy Worthen—names unknown for the most part, except for Hastings, Worthen, Craib, Pickett, and Krause, whose bylines or black and white railroad photographs appeared in print in major magazines and books of the era (see figs. 10, 11, and 13).

The place-names of city and town are plentiful too and add evocative color to the time books' yellowing pages: Duluth, Cheyenne, Denver, Durango, Reno, Laramie, Cadosia, Pomona, Los Angeles, Buffalo, and New Brunswick are penciled onto the ledger lines—destinations that were once locus points of focus, anticipation, and frenetic activity.

Figures 10, 11

Railfan photographers John Pickett with his Kodak Monitor 616, Centralia, Illinois, 1957; and Philip Hastings with his Rolleicord, Palmer, Massachusetts, 1954

Class-1 railroads get their due, with corporate initials listed too; these lull around in the margins in a jumble, forming an all-letters-of-the-alphabet roll call: NYC, PRR, NYO&W, D&H, D&RGW, CV, B&M, UP, NKP, CN, CP, DM&IR, and the SP (he photographed commuter trains in San Francisco in 1966 too). In their entirety, these notebooks are history in shorthand of an interesting chapter in American railroad photography and record memorable events in the life of one artist who made significant aesthetic contributions to its ongoing development.

Good Fortune Beyond Their Comprehension

Outlining the course and contour of one of Jim's "capers" will serve to give the reader a flavor of the adventure he found himself in. A whirlwind nine-day period in August 1956 reflects the intensity of many of his experiences.

For out-of-town trips, Jim would meet friends like Phil Hastings, Craig Woodworth, or John Pickett by either catching passenger trains such as the *Ohio State* out of Albany or by driving his own car to Canandaigua (if he was meeting Hastings) or Philadelphia (to rendezvous with Pickett). On August 17, 1956, he hit the road to Hastings's house, dutifully recording in his time books the mileage of 209 miles. In a slim column, the notation appears that he was alone on the drive, except for the occasional passing New York Central trains running on tracks flanking the highway to the south.

The next morning, Phil, John Krause, and Jim roll out of bed at 5 a.m., departing in Phil's '49 blue Pontiac. Hastings handles the driving, Krause is in the back seat, and Shaughnessy rides shotgun. The day dawns with a scattering of high clouds to the north, but it looks like the weather will be agreeably clear for photography farther west. "Barreling along" on what Shaughnessy has inscribed in his notebooks as the "August Steam Round-Up," this first day the trio will log 361 miles, finally stopping for the night in Chatham, Ontario. The morning and early afternoon will be action-packed. Hastings knows the way, having been over the same terrain with David P. Morgan a year earlier. Right after breakfast the trio covers ground across the Niagara peninsula quickly and arrives in time for early morning traffic on the CN west of Toronto at Burlington and Hamilton Junction.

After a few photos at each location (they waited about an hour at both spots), it's back in the car. Hastings, due to family and job-related responsibilities, has a schedule to keep; tarrying is not in the cards, he has to return in forty-eight hours to his psychiatric position at the Veterans Hospital in Canandaigua. Well versed in railroad operations, Phil set the frenetic pace and itinerary; Krause and Shaughnessy happily followed along. Two hours and 96 miles later they capture a diminutive

NYC 4–6–0, one of the two still operating at St. Thomas, Ontario, a division point. Laying siege to the multistall roundhouse there, Shaughnessy and Hastings clamber on and over locomotive running boards, peek into engine cabs, use the engineer's window as a frame, all the while making interesting compositions as F82-class ten-wheeler pauses among the garden tracks and then scoots into the house. Krause gets into the photography, too, with his 4 x 5. The rolls of 2¼ film Jim shot bristle with heightened intensity and enthusiasm, showing a visual curiosity and spontaneity (see pls. 46 and 74). The three photographers are juiced, inspiring and pushing each other in a friendly, competitive way. In Hastings's words, they "were fortunate beyond their comprehension."[46]

A freight train, with the other 4–6–0 (coupled to an auxiliary tender no less), is being made up in the distance. The trio piles film packs, bodies, and gear back into the car. Five dollars of regular goes into the gas tank before they depart St. Thomas. Following the train four miles out of town, they make a few shots, and then regretfully bid adieu to the diminutive consist at St. Clair Junction: Hastings has heard that Detroit, Toledo & Ironton steam might be operating in Detroit and he wants to get there, posthaste, so they won't be following the St. Clair branch. The rest of the trip west along NYC's Michigan Central mainline proves uneventful. That night in Chatham Shaughnessy's time book records $1.35 spent on a steak dinner, while a sawbuck goes toward a motel room. Before retiring for the evening, he takes twenty minutes to unload and replenish 4 x 5 film holders in a darkened bathroom, seated on the toilet, chair in front, towels over windows and door. He, along with the others, is drained but elated by the day's photo opportunities, not to mention what might come in the morning.

Next day, August 19, the three rush across the Detroit River to the outskirts of the Motor City. It's muggy. There they glimpse the cold, rusting hulks of DT&I 2–8–4s and 2–8–2s sitting forlornly by the engine house at Flat Rock yard—the locomotives Hastings had come for. Not dissuaded from the search, they drive another few hours, finding themselves south of the Ohio state line miraculously confronted by Santa Fe 2–10–4s, leased due to a surge in traffic, assisting PRR equivalents on the Columbus–Sandusky Branch near Attica Junction. Shaughnessy shoots five 4 x 5 negatives at a grade crossing; a sign advertising 7-Up frames one of the images.

Now pushing east toward home, they have lunch ($1.25), get dinged for a 40-cent toll on the Ohio Turnpike, and then stop on the B&O at Willard to shoot several frames of an ex–B&M 4–8–2 Mountain racing across the flatlands. Finally turning Hastings's Pontiac in the direction of Buffalo, they shoot a couple of Nickel Plate Berkshires, as well as a pair of Alco PAs on the evening train just outside Erie,

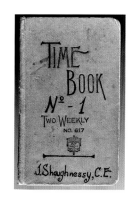

Figure 12
One of three time books Shaughnessy recorded his photography trips in. (Shaughnessy collection)

Figure 13

Illinois Central 2–10–4 #6327 poses near a water column for Ray Buhrmaster and John Pickett, Centralia, Illinois, 1957

Figure 14

Reading 4–8–4 and freight train exiting off of Rockland bridge, Harrisburg, Pennsylvania, 1956

Pennsylvania. They return to Canandaigua long after dark, pulling into Phil's driveway at 28 Park Avenue, 450 miles from where they started the day (Detroit), having dashed off 814 miles around Lake Erie in thirty-six hours. For Shaughnessy, the fun is just beginning.[47]

Next morning, August 20, he's up early, traveling alone again, on a mad dash to Philadelphia to meet John Pickett, who has a home there and works for United Airlines. He stops to fill up in Waverly, New York, puts 13.6 gallons of gas in the car for $4.50, and then takes a few photos of Lehigh Valley action south of Sayre, Pennsylvania. Pushing on through the Delaware Water Gap, he arrives in the City of Brotherly Love in the early evening, having covered 320 miles. He spends $1.20 on dinner as he and John discuss the next day's plans. It's a Friday night, and John has the weekend off. Like the trip with Hastings, this one will also be characterized by tight orchestration and lean schedules.

The duo set out the next morning, August 21, for Shenandoah, Virginia, via Harrisburg, where luckily they come across a PRR-leased Reading 4–8–4 crossing the Susquehanna over Rockville Bridge (see fig. 14 and pl. 104). Feeling fortunate, they drive on. Engaging their first Norfolk & Western steam action on the northern end of the line, they shoot in the yards at Hagerstown (see fig. 15 and pl. 19) and then at Antietam, Maryland. Hurrying to set up for a shot across the Potomac River Bridge, Shaughnessy, in an extremely rare moment, forgets to pull the dark slide as an N&W Y6b heading up a freight train rolls onto the structure—a humorous circumstance transpires (see Shaughnessy's Afterword, p. 204). The photography continues through the morning. The two stop for lunch in Shepardstown, West Virginia (60 cents), and then thread the two-lane blacktop through

a smattering of small towns in the Shenandoah Valley, reaching its namesake at nightfall. After a relaxed dinner at a local cafe ($1.60) waiting for daylight to disappear, flashbulbs and tripods get deployed, and a night photo session ensues at the engine servicing facilities and depot. Jim and John open shutters simultaneously; Pickett is only too happy to piggyback exposures to take advantage of Shaughnessy's #25 flashbulbs as Jim fires them off. They've been on the go for fourteen hours, and after the camera gear has been stowed, they find an inexpensive motel and hit the sheets.

The tempo remains fast-paced the following day, August 22. Reversing direction, they head back north to Hagerstown, shooting all the while as the N&W mainline parallels the state highways 11/340. The heavy trains run slowly through the hamlets and burgs, so even though main street traffic lights in Luray or Front Royal occasionally thwart the pair, they manage to keep abreast of northbound traffic on the railroad. They make pictures of several coal trains rolling through picturesque Virginia landscapes and past humble country stations: all of it gets recorded with the Rollei and Speed Graphic. They stop again briefly in Hagerstown in late afternoon, and then make Philadelphia by 10 p.m. that evening. Shaughnessy, ever the road warrior, is back in Troy, New York, by the evening of August 23.[48]

The morning of August 24 dawns and Shaughnessy is again behind the wheel, heading to Montreal. He meets Sandy Worthen there, crashing for the night on his friend's couch. They do a day of train photography around the city on the twenty-fifth, hitting the Glen engine terminal and spots along the western lakeshore, where both CN and CP mainlines ran. On the twenty-sixth, he again drives the 239 miles home to Troy. Over the span of nine days he's covered

almost 2,600 miles, and been in two countries and seven states. This dynamic pattern of photographic activity was the norm for Shaughnessy throughout the 1950s, as he scurried to record steam's curtain call. Carpe diem, it seems, was a mandate he took seriously.

The Railroad in Its Everyday Work Clothes: A Photography Open to Possibilities

The railroad photography world Shaughnessy entered was in need of an aesthetic overhaul, if not outright scrapping. As has been documented elsewhere (see *A Passion for Trains*, W. W. Norton, 2004, pp. 9–11), the three-quarter wedge aesthetic (as practiced and promoted by Lucius Beebe) ruled the pictorial roost in the 1930s, 1940s, and early 1950s and became the default approach employed by most railfan photographers during this era. While this style predominated in the pages of the leading magazines of the day, such as *Trains* and *Railroad*, Shaughnessy never consciously adopted it, although he wasn't opposed to it and would sometimes make a wedge shot "for the record if the light were right" (see pl. 38).

He was self-taught and, like many artists, had only an inkling as to where the reference points for his developing photographic skills

originated (see above, p. 14). His early negatives from 1946–50 nonetheless indicate an openness to a different vision (how many photographers were taking photographs from locomotive cabs in 1946? see fig. 5). They also show an occasional interest in "atmospherics" (see figs. 17, 18, and pl. 135)—a trait that soon shifts instead toward a clear delineation and accurate rendering of what was before the camera.

Photography is a contest between a photographer and the presumptions of approximate and habitual seeing. The contest can be held anywhere.
—John Szarkowski[49]

Figure 15

Engineer oils around, Norfolk & Western, Hagerstown, Maryland, 1956

Figure 16

Norfolk & Western freight with 2–6–6–4 A-class locomotive, east of Roanoke, Virginia, 1956

By looking at
pictures you learn.
—Jim Shaughnessy[50]

Figure 17

Delaware & Hudson
4–6–6–4 on freight train,
Watervliet, New York,
1950

Figure 18

Rutland *Green Mountain
Flyer* with 4–8–2 #92
pulls into Union Station,
Troy, New York,
1949

While he shied away from the other standard practices of the day—taking roster shots, and the trading and selling of negatives and postcard-sized prints via the International Engine Picture Club—Shaughnessy does recall being interested in the mechanical aspects of locomotives. Here he saw a pictorial quality in close-ups of rods or crossheads that made for striking industrial images (see fig. 20). He liked what he saw within the overall railroad environment too, and found many of its elements "beautiful or worth taking a photo of."[51] Equally, and most importantly, he wanted to capture the railroad "as it presented itself," trusting there "would be enough variety in equipment, lighting, human interaction or situation to make the photography interesting."[52] Though his creative and aesthetic ambitions remained modest, his drive to actually do the photography was anything but, as his extensive archive and notebooks attest.

The major accomplishment of Jim's photography was to depict how things looked within urban townscapes, cities, and rural topographies of the Northeast in that important transitional period for America's railroad culture, the 1950s. His thoughtful, content-filled compositions capture a sense of place *and* a sense of time, describing in well-observed moments how the engines, railroaders, terminals, yards, outbuildings, station architecture, and landscape looked.

"Photography," as Lee Friedlander has said, "is a generous medium" and "usually there's more in the frame than we realize when taking the picture."[53] By aiming the camera at the world, and maintaining an open-door policy toward content, Shaughnessy took advantage of photography's information-gathering capabilities. This, then, was the value of pulling back from the trains to contextualize them and going "environmental" (a term coined by writers and railfans Tony Reevy

and Greg McDonnell[54]). Pictures showing track with rock ballast (or lack thereof), a gaggle of baggage carts languishing near the station with Railway Express Agency trucks in the background, the complex weave of freight yard tracks, or the socioeconomic implications of warehouses or tenements adjacent to the rail line create a broader understanding for the viewer of railroading's visual culture. These scenes also allow us to see (and analyze) the interconnections between the railroad and its environs (see figs. 2, 3, 4, 5, and 18).

If Shaughnessy had maintained a closed-off perspective, as Beebe had earlier in his career (Beebe's own photography later become less conventional and more artistic; see *Age of Steam,* Howell–North, 1957, p. 196), future historians, rail preservationists, or modelers might never have known how a NYC RS3 looked as it threaded through the densely packed industrial settings of downtown Troy (see fig. 19). We might not be able to imagine how closely a depot was configured into a cityscape, or know how Manhattan's skyline looked looming behind a New York Central road switcher paused on the High Line on the city's West Side—or how that anomalous piece of urban railroad architecture actually appeared (see pl. 50).

Indicative of the value of Jim's work is the fact that RPI's model railroad club, one of the nation's oldest such organizations, has mined Jim's photographic archive over the last twenty years to help re-create a historically accurate replica of Troy, New York, and its environs, circa 1957, as well as myriad locations along the D&H's mainline around the Empire State. Similarly, New York City's Save the High Line Committee (an organization working on its redevelopment) used Jim's photos on its Web site, and in videos and articles, to raise public awareness for the project,[55] and two of Shaughnessy's images

Figure 19

New York Central
Alco RS3s on wye,
Troy, New York,
1955

Figure 20

Driving wheels and
connecting rods of
Canadian Pacific
4–6–2 locomotive
Three Rivers, Quebec,
1956

Figure 21

Delaware & Hudson
brakeman signals
on top of boxcar,
Colonie yard,
near Watervliet,
New York,
1961

were used to open a short documentary narrated by the actor Edward Norton.[56] That these two diverse organizations can rely on the visual record Shaughnessy created is a testament to the comprehensiveness of his archives and the inclusive nature of his photographs.

The different types of photographs Shaughnessy made and passed on stylistically to second-generation railfan photographers reflect not only his careful observation of railroading but also the influence of his scientific background, his love of history, his choice of photographic equipment, and his personal predilections for certain terrains. The theories that follow spring from my exposure to his in-print work over the last five decades, as well as my impressions after reviewing his entire black-and-white negative archive since 1945, approximately 60,000 images—a viewing that unearthed the rare and the typical.

The keepers and the outtakes speak volumes, telling much about intention, direction, likes, and dislikes. Repeated motifs inevitably occur. "Every artist's work," as the graphic designer Rudy Vanderlans has suggested, "eventually matures into a distinctive look,"[57] and Jim's did as well. If he tried a certain technique or style of picture, and it worked, he used it again and again as any artist might. The same went for the many landscapes and locations he ventured into around the Albany/Troy area. He made hundreds of images at the Cohoes Bridge, the D&H's Colonie shops, Mechanicville yard, or Coon's Crossing on the B&M—all within thirty minutes of his home. Repeatedly returning to these familiar locales, he never got bored and always found the lighting conditions, situation, or equipment going by unique and worthy of his attention.[58]

Throughout his career he applied various photographic styles to what he did. These multifaceted approaches were perhaps influenced by the numerous commercial/industrial jobs (rail-related and non-rail-related) he did in Troy and around New York state for clients between 1955 and 1990, shooting everything from weddings, to office buildings, to new gas stations, to piggyback trains for *Railway Age* (he did a story on the New York Central's Flexi-van service in 1957). For instance, the photograph from 1961 of brakeman Paul Mooney on top of a boxcar (or throwing a switch) at the Colonie yard (see fig. 21 and pl. 16) is staged in a way that resembles annual report imagery created by Chicago's Hedrich–Blessing firm during the same era (see *Starlight on the Rails*, Abrams, 2000, p. 97). This approach made sense based on the equipment—using a 4 x 5 is a cumbersome process; photographer and subject would have been aware of one another, and cooperative in taking the photograph. Spontaneity was not the point; but an accurate, clear rendering, illustrating an idea, was. The fact that only one frame was exposed for each image suggests that Shaughnessy took a deliberate, no-nonsense, journeyman-like approach to making his photographs.[59] Confidently, he exposed one sheet of film and felt self-assured enough to have gotten an image he deemed satisfactorily representative of the scene.

Sometimes he appropriated the compositional ideas and pictorial cues of traditional "camera club" landscape photography (he occasionally worked for *Adirondack Life* and *Downeast* magazines, writing articles with historical photos included, but perhaps his exposure to these magazines in general influenced these pictorial decisions). He would often bring his own spirea bushes or forsythia branches along to border the picture frame, adding foliage to the foreground—a trick he learned from Gene Baxter, another local Troy photographer (see *Trains*, May 1953, p. 31, for an image by Baxter).[60]

In evaluating the emotional content of his photos, it seems that Jim was never overly interested in nostalgia or sentiment; rather, as someone with a left-brain, scientific orientation, he might see such images as inaccurate representations or impressions of the past. The historian's hat he often wore while shooting instilled an appreciation for the historical significance of whatever was before his lens (a steam locomotive, let's say). However, I sense that he also realized he was shooting said locomotive in real time and not as an industrial relic to be fawned over at some future date. (Walker Evans called this attitude an awareness of "the historical contemporary" and thought nostalgia "a fuzzy representation of the past"—ideas with which Jim would concur.)[63] During the course of our interviews Jim never alluded to feeling overt sadness about steam's demise, as Steinheimer had, which may account for Steinheimer's more frequent use of emotional content and elegy versus Shaughnessy's objective, distanced stance.

Jim accepted historic progression and entropy as natural processes in the world of railroading, and never became acrimonious over the changes that occurred within the industry. (This attitude has served him well; he's actively making railroad photographs in 2007.) When he recorded, for instance, the demolition of Troy's Union depot in 1958, the photographs appear as factual documents of a specific event, not as statements of ineffable loss. Shots of Southern Pacific RSD5s being scrapped in Albany (see pl. 59), or the skeletal remains of the Central Vermont's train shed trusses laid aground in St. Albans (see pl. 119), are eerily reminiscent of George Barnard's dispassionate Civil War images depicting the destruction of Atlanta after Sherman's scorched-earth "march to the sea" in 1864[64]—important historical documents as well as artful ones.

For the record, however, neither approach (emotionalism or objectivity) trumps the other. Important schools of photography, such as Germany's *Neue Sachlichkeit* (New Objectivity) from the 1920s, eschewed any sense of expressionism in a photograph, stressing instead "the materiality of substances [photographed] rather than the maker's emotional attitude toward the subject." The New Objectivists were interested in the "matter-of-factness" of things. Members of this influential group, among them Albert Renger-Patzsch, "believed that the final image should exist in all its completeness before the exposure was made and that it should be an un-manipulated record."[65] Shaughnessy instinctively adhered to these tenets. That he practiced a philosophy of objectivity in his photography isn't stretching; he said he wanted to photograph the railroad "the way it was" and not the way he felt or thought about it. He also made straight prints of images he previsualized in-camera before tripping the shutter, mirroring Renger-Patzsch's philosophy of completeness. The cropping of

negatives, and minor burning and dodging while printing, seem to be the only darkroom manipulations he allowed himself; he never became overly involved in the Ansel Adams "the negative is the score, and the print is the performance" type of attitude. To this day he has a utilitarian, nonfussy approach when making prints, a trait Walker Evans shared (to a degree) and would have approved of.

Five Aspects Discussed

The photographic ideas I'll discuss about the type of pictures Shaughnessy made are part of the canon of twentieth-century photography, and thus applicable when talking about his work. Five kinds of images come to mind: 1) staged or directed photography, where the photographer attempts to re-create an image he's seen in his mind and purposely poses engine or worker to capture the tableau on film; 2) night photography, where using various flash techniques adds drama to a railroad situation that might appear lifeless in daylight; 3) participatory photography, where the viewer and photographer's experiences merge to create the sensation of "being there"; 4) human-interest photography, where people are included in the frame to explore relationships between man and his environment— in this case, the railroad scene; 5) sense of place (and time) photography, where the medium's descriptive powers are utilized for historical and cultural documentation. These kinds of photographs were regularly made by Shaughnessy and others as part of a new visual language emerging between train photographers and the railroad landscape they encountered in the late 1940s and early 1950s. These artists wanted to expand upon what got recorded as part of railroading visual culture. The word "landscape" here refers to everything related to railroading; "visual culture" refers to what can be seen.

1. The Staged Image: Art Director in the Yards

Without question, the leading examples of the staged photograph in rail-centered photography during the past half century were the images O. Winston Link composed on the N&W between 1955 and 1960. But Shaughnessy decided, before knowing of Link's work, to combine open-flash and existing light with simple staging when doing night photography too. He said recently that a Steinheimer image from Saugus, California, of a Southern Pacific 2–10–2 with two trainmen posing, engine in the foreground, water tank in the background (see *Trains*, August 1952, pp. 38–39), was a frame of reference for his initial foray into night and staged photography. An "I'd-like-to-see-if-I-could-do-that-too" attitude ensued (see figs. 22 and 24).

This type of photography allowed him to behave like a film director previsualizing, deciding ahead of time the contents of the frame, concurrently thinking how the image might appear as a final print or reproduction in a magazine. He placed a strong emphasis on "seeing the image before exposing the film."[66] His engineering orientation probably influenced this approach; he didn't want to operate in a zone of happenstance, preferring to control the outcome as best he could. Scrutinizing his work—such as the image of two Canadian National employees at the Brockville, Ontario, engine facilities (see fig. 24), or the impressive shots of Rutland milk trains (see figs. 23 and pl. 101) hanging high over the Walloomsac River in Rensselaer County, New York, in 1959, which he orchestrated with the railroad, a handheld fusee, flashbulbs, and a cadre of friends—we begin to appreciate what Shaughnessy was after. These photographs, though posed, come across in a casual way, suggesting he was striving for spontaneity and naturalism.

During the 1950s, when a photograph's veracity was rarely challenged in academic circles or the media, Shaughnessy felt shy about revealing the contrived nature of these images—he wanted viewers to accept them as reality, and he didn't want to spoil the illusion. However, he routinely posed locomotives and whole trains, or used family and friends as props for his images. (His wife, Carol, and friend John Pickett appear as passengers, his father as a station agent at Mount Holly, Vermont. See *Night Train*, Pacific Railway Journal, 1961, pp. 98 and 104, or pl. 51 here.) Ironically, this style of photography (the "staged" photograph) is now the zeitgeist in contemporary American photography, as practiced by Jeff Wall, Gregory Crewdson, Philip Lorca diCorcia, Justin Kurland, and a host of other photographers who believe that all photographs are mediated events anyway, regardless of the photographer's intentions. Shaughnessy was ahead of the curve in a modest way, and can be considered, along with Link, a historical precursor to this contemporary practice.

Despite their "staged-to-re-create-a-reality-once-seen" aspect, Jim's photos give us accurate depictions of railroading realities in the 1950s and 1960s. Does it matter that he interjected a little authorial presence in order to give us the essence of what he was trying to convey? If the scene had been unsullied by any human interference, is the inherent truth or reality of the photograph any greater? I don't think it matters; they come across as artful and honest representations of the "railroad in its everyday work clothes,"[67] which matched Shaughnessy's stated intention.

2. Night Photography: Flashes in the After-Dark

Dramatic nighttime locomotive or train portraits, made around freight yards, on ready-tracks, on bridges, or in (or near) engine houses or

Figure 22

Shaughnessy lighting a locomotive with open flash using 25 flashbulbs. Photograph by Curt Law 1956

Figure 23

Rutland freight train with RS3 #206 on high bridge across Walloomsac River, North Hoosick, New York, 1959

Figure 24

Canadian National 4–8–4 #6258 on ready track with two crew members awaiting orders, Brockville, Ontario, 1958

roundhouses, also became part of the Shaughnessy signature style. "I seem to be having some luck with this after-dark stuff," he told *Trains* editors in the November 1955 issue (page 33). These places acted as open-air studios where Jim could arrange interesting steam/diesel juxtapositions. The exciting part of photographing around engine terminals was the fluctuating action that might portend drama. Wait fifteen minutes and a different locomotive—fresh off one run or being readied for another—could present itself before the lens. For Jim, something analogous to a theatrical performance was going on; the architecture, ambient light, locomotives, and railroad personnel were elements in a play, set on a vast, moody industrial stage. This ever-shifting array of movement, equipment, and possibility made such locations Shaughnessy favorites and suggest why engine portraits constitute such a large body of his night work. His visceral appreciation for this close proximity to such marvels of the mechanical age is evident too. For Jim, a locomotive was a "vision of power, beauty, order and purpose."[68] He wanted to photograph them in an unconventional way, highlighting their heroic proportions and mien. He became (in the words of Lucius Beebe) "a photographer skilled in the technique of night lighting and the massive effects of black and white."[69]

With the constraints of slow film speeds, reciprocity failure, and bulky 4 x 5 equipment within a dark industrial environment, Shaughnessy felt it necessary to paint with flash instead of depending solely on available light when trying to capture the essence of the scene. He employed bayonet and screw-mounted flashbulbs of the #5, #25, #11, #22, and #50 sizes, the egg-shaped #25 being the favored choice for portability and output. When a "big gun" was necessary for intense illumination and wattage (as with the Rutland trestle photos), the #50 was used to cover larger areas.

The painted approach went like this: after composing the scene, Jim would open the shutter and then walk around painting and filling in with light from his flash gun. A friend might accompany him on the shoot and, if the overall exposure was a little long due to a large area needing coverage, Jim—with an agreed-upon signal—would alert his assistant to place a dark slide in front of the lens momentarily to prevent too much ambient light from burning into the negatives' highlights. He then continued on, firing off his number #25 flashbulbs in the darkness, to complete the exposure.[70] Focusing was done using the lens's hyper-focal calibrations, with an f8 or 11 aperture the norm when using Kodak Royal Pan 400, his preferred film choice.

This painted flash approach is still the preferred modus operandi for the majority of railfans making night images today, and the method used by earlier Shaughnessy contemporaries like Richard Steinheimer and Robert Hale. This includes a large East Coast

contingent that pays homage to the lessons imparted by Shaughnessy and Link. Led by Jim Boyd, former editor of *Railfan* magazine—and a talented photographer in his own right who has done over a hundred setups since 1968—this group democratized night photo sessions by making them into "events."[71] While this cadre of railfans shares with the older photographers a penchant for flash photography, gritty rail environments, and rural tableaux, they don't depend on Link-like synchronized stop-action extravaganzas; rather, the majority of their image making relies on the Shaughnessy method of open flash, time exposure, and staged trains or locomotives at rest. His influence has clearly been pervasive in this regard.

Shaughnessy did synchronized "light-up-the-night" photography for a handful of pictures, the first in 1951 (see fig. 25, which predates Link's work by four years); he even once contemplated constructing an elaborate battery-capacitor flash unit like the one Link used to stop action,[72] but soon jettisoned the idea for an approach pared to thrift and simplicity: available light, time exposure, and "painted" open flash. Flash photography was done with either a handheld Graphflex unit or, in the case of the Rutland pictures (see pls. 57 and 101), a homemade collection of reflectors fashioned from pie tins attached to tree limbs or light stands with clamps. Lamp wire purchased from the local hardware store strung everything together.

In April 1956, on one of the several trips Shaughnessy made with Phil Hastings, the two stopped in Brattleboro, Vermont, to make a series of images at the Central Vermont roundhouse on the eve of a B&M #3713 excursion run, in which Jim would go on to create perhaps his most memorable image (see pl. 43 as well as *Trains*, August 1983, p. 45). With time to kill, the two photographers, aided by a friendly hostler who spotted CV 0-8-0 switcher #501 on the turntable, employed the open-flash, time exposure method, shooting well past midnight (see pl. 86). The two men sometimes set up their tripods near each other, but Shaughnessy alone handled the flash duties.[73] In fact, Jim recalls that on all the trips he made with Hastings, he supervised the lighting. That Hastings deferred to his companion in this regard, despite the fact that he himself had been employing time exposures and open flash as early as 1950,[74] is a testament to Shaughnessy's artistic prowess with artificial illumination.

3. The Participatory Image: Viewer Involvement

Viewer involvement would become a recognizable component in some of Shaughnessy's work too—you felt as though you were inside the experience with him, drawn into the act of creation, or actually standing in the environment he originally inhabited. The invention and dissemination of photojournalism's "in-your-face, you-are-there" style,

Figure 25
Shaughnessy's first synchronized flash photograph of New York Central 2-8-2 #3754, Troy, New York, 1951

Figure 26
Wabash F7A #1160 and CN 2-8-2 #3431, Fort Erie, Ontario, 1956

which originated in the late 1920s in Europe and blossomed fully throughout the American print media in the 1930s, 1940s, 1950s, brought a new immediacy and freedom to photographic images and decreed that the reality in front of the camera might merge with the photographer's artistic intentions to dictate how the picture got made. Jim, being naturally curious and open to experimentation, appropriated various tactics in the service of his rail photography "to try something new." When seeing a photo of this kind, the viewer might feel the breathtaking sprint of a Boston & Maine 4–6–2 galloping across the film plane near Haverhill, Massachusetts (see pl. 43); become enveloped, along with the photographer and his Speed Graphic, by a blizzard engulfing Troy's Union depot, as a crossing guard signals to the switch engine assembling a train (see pl. 33); or be leaning over the engineer's shoulder, looking down the CP mainline, as the 4–6–0 quick-changes the landscape across the prairies of Ontario (see pl. 83).

Shaughnessy's numerous pacing images, perhaps influenced by a bevy of photographers such as Robert Hale, J. Parker Lamb, David Conner, A. C. Kalmbach, and Francis Le Jaques[75] (as seen in early-1950s issues of *Trains*), also have a participatory feel. Shaughnessy wanted to capture, in a still frame, the sensation of movement and visceral experience he had while riding in a car chasing a locomotive or train at speed. Based on his repeated success with this type of photograph (he made hundreds of negatives in this mode), Shaughnessy's images come across as quintessential examples of this technique (see fig. 1 and pls. 8, 35, 116, and 127), perhaps trumping Hale's best efforts.

Unusual angles came into play as well. A camera placed at rail level (see pls. 107 and 131), from an aerial perspective (see fig. 2 and pl. 113), or positioned in a spot usually not accessible to a photographer on the ground (see pl. 84) also opened different aesthetic doors, offering new opportunities of perception about how railroading might be depicted, framed, and "looked" at.

4. Human Interest: A Vital Component Adding to the Scene

Photojournalism also introduced railfan photographers to the notion that people in general, and railroad employees in particular, could become key elements within their compositions. Portraits and iconographic images of workers, in situ or isolated and made heroic within their environment, but not divorced from it, became part of the canon. Suddenly, train shooters like Shaughnessy understood that this man/machine interaction might be a visual enhancement.

The inclusion of workers in photographs may have also derived from the restless curiosity of cameramen seeking a broader visual knowledge of their subject matter—they wanted to focus their lenses on something other than the hardware. The steam era was fading,

and with its demise inherent pictorial qualities singular to that technology vanished. Many lensmen felt the diesels' standardized sterility was no match for the visual allure of steam. Subsequently, these image makers thought that by placing human beings within their frames they could recapture, for their rail photography, some of vitality and excitement steam had lent to the scene. Or perhaps the realization that many vocations on the railroad were soon to be obsolete due to technological evolution proved to be a motivating factor in getting photographers to film workers whose jobs were in jeopardy.

The human element also broadened the narrative possibilities in rail photography. Jim took advantage of this by placing workers in his photographs, but it was rarely in the service of constructing a story line about a particular person; this wasn't his style. That being said, his archive does contain one photo story, shot exclusively on 2¼ film in June 1957, which he proposed to *Trains*—on a D&H railroader by the name of Henry Stewart. Unfortunately, it never ran and the close-up portrait of Stewart is an atypical image in his file (see fig. 27).[76]

Shaughnessy's photographs incorporating members of the railroad's workforce were never about the men per se. They were about the interaction between the machines, the men (switchmen, brakemen, operators, conductors, or engineers), and the railroad landscape. The locomotives, trains, geography, and work environment for the most part were given equal weight within the picture space, with the laborers usually (but not always) relegated to a friendly anonymity. That doesn't mean he didn't deem them important. While Jim wanted to show that railroaders were essential to the industry, he usually chose not to feature them prominently, or boldly frontal, as Ted Benson might have (see *One Track Mind,* Boston Mills Press, 1999, pp. 13, 123, 128). We get a sense of what the worker did, how he fit into the scheme of things, without knowing the employee in a personal way. It may have been easier to round up models in any situation, too, precisely because they weren't to be in the foreground, or they would appear in shadow, or have their backs to the camera (see fig. 29 and pls. 9, 12, 13, 14, 19, 20, 29, 30, 36, 61, 71, 73, 96, and 111). Perhaps the brakeman or hostler didn't want to be recognized for fear of reprisals if management ever saw the image in print but enjoyed cooperating with someone fascinated by his profession nonetheless.

When Shaughnessy did focus on an individual, the rail worker depicted could be considered a quintessential representation. A case in point is the portrait of D&H brakeman Paul Mooney (see pl. 16). Lucius Beebe used this picture as proxy, transforming Mooney into an employee of the Southern Pacific in the Sierra foothills (see *The Central Pacific and Southern Pacific Railroads*, Howell–North, 1963, p. 272). Beebe liked the photograph, needed human interest for the book, and took artistic license when writing the caption.

Figure 27
Portrait of Delaware & Hudson engineer Henry Stewart inside cab of Alco RS3, Whitehall, New York, 1957

Its out-of-context placement illustrates how Shaughnessy's distanced, dispassionate stance lent a sense of universality or even "everyman-ness" to the image, while a more personal portrayal might have failed because of its specificity. This usage fit Beebe's needs perfectly, while also showing that Shaughnessy's brand of industrial-image making had stock photography applications. In fact, Jim was a favored contributor to Beebe's books; his work appeared in eight of them.[77]

On a personal note, Jim by nature isn't intrusive. Even the mild direction he gave to railroaders while making his photographs was always done with the respect and knowledge that they were actually working. He didn't want to delay them or take up their time unnecessarily. This attitude explains why only one or two frames of any given situation ever got made.

5. Sense of Place, Sense of Time: The Historical and Cultural Document

Capturing a sense of place, a sense of geographic space, or a sense of time in an image, too, was essentially a by-product of Shaughnessy's inquisitive photographic habits. He paid attention to the total railroad scene, shooting the physical plant and surrounding environment as well as the trains. By including fragments of roundhouses and depots, or swathes of distant fields and large-scale pastoral scenes—or by including elements like signage and automobiles that anchor a picture in time—Jim inevitably made records of now-vanished places, "fallen-flag" landscapes, and lost locomotives. The photographs act as historical documents of what was there, in a way a tightly framed Beebe three-quarter shot never completely could.

Shaughnessy and other photographers also started paying more attention to the railroads' interior life. Their curiosity drove them inside, to stations, telegrapher's bays, and locomotive shops; no place was off-limits to their imaginations or Speed Graphics. Shaughnessy, throughout his travels, gained privileged access to many railroad environments. The impact of this can't be overemphasized. The social climate in the 1950s, far removed from the suspicious, liability-sensitive post–9/11 environment we inhabit today, was more user-friendly. Railfans were tacitly welcomed on railroad property by blue-collar workers, but told to "take your pictures, be careful, and look out for the guys in white hats" (supervisors). In some cases, railfans were able to sign waivers that absolved the railroad company from legal responsibility while they were on the property. Shaughnessy notes that Paducah, Kentucky, on the Illinois Central, home to its major repair shop and engine-servicing facility, was one such location.[78]

This arrangement afforded the average railfan photographer myriad photo opportunities, as the infrastructure needed to keep the trains running then—the backshops, erecting floors, roundhouse bays, and locomotive pits—was more extensive (and manned by more personnel doing interesting and specialized jobs). This also partially accounts for why railroading and railroad photography fifty years ago was more visually compelling than today: aesthetically pleasing subject matter was more abundant and available to shoot. Jim Boyd recently described this 1950s railroad landscape as "a target-rich environment," which seems apt.[79] It's interesting to ponder, too, the what-ifs. What if this kind of access hadn't been available to Shaughnessy and his contemporaries? The photographic record of mid-century railroading (and the sense of what these places looked and felt like) would be that much poorer, and future historians would have had a difficult time understanding, in a visual way, what went on behind the closed doors of America's railroads.

The Lay of the Land: The Railroad Landscape of the Northeast in the 1950s

In the years of Shaughnessy's childhood, the quaint New England rural countryside remained constant, especially in places like western Vermont, the upper Champlain Valley, New Hampshire, or along the Canadian borderlands. Many locations lingered as isolated backwaters, never able to attract much industry or development. Marble quarrying, lumbering, dairy farming, and textile manufacturing put products on the rails, but as the "American economy took on a wild urgency in its shift from an agricultural to industrial base"[80] (a trend that began in the late nineteenth century), many railroads of the Northeast got left out of the boom. Small towns and manufacturing centers eventually became depopulated as corporations, seeking cheap labor and tax relief, moved south and west. Workers followed, hoping to find better living conditions and employment opportunities in Sunbelt cities.

This transition was reflected in the railroad landscape of the 1950s. Many railroads went to the same places with redundant trackage, were burdened with too many branch lines that served small industries generating too few carloads, and were battling with truckers for the same scarce shipments. On top of this, the future lay not in piecemeal freight traffic generated by small line-side customers but in the long-haul bulk commodities generated by major industries. Many railroads had either money-losing commuter passenger service on mainlines or money-losing passenger service on local trains; ridership was lean, the losses unsustainable, and the equipment in deteriorating condition.

Getting freight in or out of the Northeast was also a challenge. Even with five bridges straddling the Hudson in New York— at Poughkeepsie, Castleton, Albany, and Mechanicville—significant percentages of traffic moved via tugboat or barge. Oftentimes,

Figure 28
Derailment of the Rutland's *Mount Royal* passenger train, Arlington, Vermont, 1949

circuitous routes were required to get the freight to its destination.[82] Several roads struggled with poor management and troubling finances; many railroads in the Northeast had been in receivership at least once in the past century.[83] Deferred maintenance of aging physical plants and trackage beaten down during World War II's overuse of the nation's railroad infrastructure was the norm, too, and proved problematic.

The fact was that the railroads were paying the price for a century of unfettered build-out, where rails went "from nowhere to nowhere" in a region that had lost what small industrial base it had. The economics could no longer support so many individual railroad enterprises. Insulting the already injured, the government-funded interstate highway system was signed into law in 1956—another kind of death knell for the area's railroads. While freight began migrating to trucks as early as the 1920s (as roads improved in rural areas and trucks reached out for the short-haul, small-town, less-than-carload business),[84] new highways and interstates built thirty years later went many places more directly, costing the railroads their competitive edge. Standardization and modernization within the railroad industry was taking hold everywhere with the introduction of labor-reducing, fuel-saving diesel locomotives, centralized traffic control, and streamlined passenger trains to try and stave off the citizenry's mass migration to the automobile and airplane.

With this reconfiguration of the railroad landscape, many of the eastern carriers Jim knew intimately were on life support, in the final throes of reorganization, or trying desperately to shore up shaky financial performance before abandonment. If outright abandonment didn't occur, contraction and merger were evident everywhere.

Cases in point: in Shaughnessy's hometown, the Troy depot succumbed to the wrecking ball in 1958; the Rutland, due to unresolved labor negotiations and track redundancy, closed shop in 1961. Railroads like the New York, Ontario & Western died right before his eyes in 1957, the nail already in its coffin as he captured gray and yellow FTs leading a freight south at Kerryville, New York, one year earlier (see pl. 66). Shaughnessy also saw the Penn Central petition to abandon its Elmira Branch—a last bastion for steaming class I-1 2–10–0 Decapods and a bucolic stretch of track running between Williamsport, Pennsylvania, and Sodus Point, New York—after the devastating effects of Hurricane Agnes in 1972; five years earlier the coal docks at the northern end of the line had suspended operation. The flags of the NYC, B&M, Rutland, and the NYO&W would wave, fall to half-mast fluttering, and then disappear outright (see fig. 29) within the first thirty years of Shaughnessy's photographic journey.[85]

In what Richard Saunders has termed "the golden glow years" (1945–55) of American railroading,[86] Jim saw the demise of passenger trains (passenger traffic peaked on the Rutland in 1924,[87] typical of

many railroads) and the end of steam (nationally, steam locomotives hauled 78 percent of freight in 1946, 31 percent in 1951, and 0.5 percent in 1959).[88] He took pictures that spoke of a bright future for railroading that never materialized (his photographs of NYC's *Aerotrain* come to mind; see fig. 31). He watched as diesels arrived, encroaching into freight yards and roundhouses, decimating the rank-and-file U.S. railroad workforce, whose numbers fell from a high of approximately 2,100,000 in the early 1920s to 1,400,000 in 1945, to a paltry 500,000 in 1975.[89]

Shaughnessy captured most of the railroads of this far-flung eastern rail empire: the Class-1 trunk lines, the Anthracite and Pocahontas roads, the New England bridge lines, the CN and CP in southern Canada, and the quaint, ubiquitous short lines he had a special fondness for that seemed to spring from everywhere. Even Midwestern bridge lines that roamed "the heartland of American manufacturing" landed on his sheets of film. Later, this proclivity for all-encompassing coverage included less familiar quadrants of the country—the western and northern plains and the mountainous regions of the Southwest—where he eventually photographed the Union Pacific, Great Northern, Colorado & Southern, Duluth, Missabe & Iron Range, and the Rio Grande narrow gauge. He even twice traveled to Mexico in the early 1960s to document the picturesque steam locomotives there, when their brethren had all but vanished from North America.

End Times—But Good Times Still Rolling

Witnessing the final flowering, then wilting, of steam power in America only to see the scene morph into a homogenized, dieselized landscape should have been a letdown for Shaughnessy. By taking it in stride, however, keeping his sentiment in check and never growing maudlin, Jim remained a pragmatic observer of American railroading. He accepted this technological change with equilibrium and even developed an intense curiosity about the Diesel.

With this erosion of "color" on the railroad (in terms of interesting locomotives, infrastructure, and support systems), he might have felt the rail scene offered less opportunity for artistic exploration. It would have been easy to set aside the cameras, as many of his contemporaries had. Instead, he shifted gears and became acclimatized to a new world order. Like an industrial archaeologist gathering forensic evidence, Jim became more wedded to the straight documentary tradition in his photography during the late 1960s and early 1970s. With marriage (in 1961) to Carol MacNaughton, the inclusion of eighty-seven of his images in Donald Duke's *Night Train* (Pacific Railway Journal, San Marino, 1961; see fig. 30), and the completion of the *Rutland Road* and *Delaware and Hudson* books (Howell–North, Berkeley, 1964 and

The Rutland had few factories in the sleepy little villages that dotted its routemap. Its people were not for the most part factory hands but small independent farmers, purchasers not producers. Without them fully realizing it, the great surge of industrial progress was passing them by in high gear.

—Jim Shaughnessy,
The Rutland Road[81]

Figure 29

New York, Ontario & Western Railroad brakeman and NW2 #122 in freight yard, Middletown, New York, 1957

1967, respectively; reprinted Syracuse University Press, 1997) a "been there, done that" attitude may have prevailed. In addition, with the birth of James Jr. in 1974, his priorities undoubtedly changed.

With less time to devote to the hobby or to long-distance travel, the archive shows Jim staying closer to home. Mechanicville became his mecca, where round-the-clock activity within the B&M and D&H engine facilities, sanding towers, and yards provided ample photographic opportunities. Even though he'd always been an eager participant in railfan excursions, this type of activity got more of his attention in the 1960s, 1970s, and 1980s too (confirming his interest in preservation as well). David P. Morgan often dispatched Jim trackside to cover first runs for *Trains*. Since Jim liked getting ink in "The Magazine of Railroading" he was only too happy to oblige. While occasional sheets of 4 x 5 got shot, a newly acquired Mamiya RB67 handled the bulk of the photography during this period.

Behind him were the great trips into the Canadian provinces, the far West, the near Midwest, the Virginias, and Mexico (see figs. 16 and 34). He had conducted his own steam safaris throughout the 1950s, concurrent with the activities of Hastings and Morgan, covering some of the same ground. (In fact, Jim introduced Hastings to the PRR's Elmira Branch in May 1957; some of those Hastings images became the basis of a *Trains* article in November of that year.) In this earlier period—from 1947 through his final trip to Mexico in 1962—the allure of steam acted as the propellant driving his interests. After 1970, however, a deepening fascination with diesel technology, coupled with an ongoing inquisitiveness about contemporary railroading's evolving history, carried him forward.

Embracing this new mind-set, over the next twenty years Shaughnessy made thousands of builder-like diesel images in and around the Colonie shops—pictures reminiscent of those acquired by H. L. Broadbelt from Alco and other locomotive manufacturers (see fig. 32). It was a collection he was familiar with and admired.[90] This is ironic, considering his nonparticipation in the Engine Picture Club during the 1940s and the roster-shot style of photography it promoted. Perhaps as he matured, with life inevitably taking on different meanings, making uninflected visual records of railroad equipment for posterity became important.

It's not that he hadn't done this in the past: the documentary tradition had long been integral to his approach, often running in tandem with his more creative efforts. Even here he was characteristically tireless; he duly recorded every eventuality that occurred on his hometown railroads—from derailments (fig. 28) to buildings being demolished, to engines being scrapped, to engines being rebuilt, to circus trains arriving, to mainlines being abandoned, to whole railroads shuttered by strikes. He even photographed part of the set for the film

Ironweed, starring Jack Nicholson and Meryl Streep, shot in the Schenectady/Albany area in 1987. He became the de facto archivist and cataloger of the local railroad scene. He relished the role.

Shaughnessy made the best of it by focusing (reverentially) in his later years on esoteric diesels that the D&H acquired during the Carl B. Sterzling era (the Baldwin Sharks and the Alco PA's got extensive coverage).[91] He became "the man" on the property, with an official pass to roam mainlines, shops, and yards at will. The company might stop the *Laurentian* (for him and his camera) along the banks of Lake Champlain (see fig. 37); pose three freshly out-shopped PA's in front of Colonie's diesel shop (see pl. 41); or hold freight trains on its affiliate Erie Lackawanna line high atop Starrucca Viaduct, as a brother D&H freight train passed below (see pl. 79). He enjoyed this new-found position as unofficial company photographer for the D&H, an honor bestowed after the publication of his landmark history of that railroad in 1967.

Finally, too, he could rest on his laurels and survey the fruits of his labor. Over his five decades of rail photography, Jim had exposed 120,000 sheets or frames of film, in sizes ranging from 35mm to 4 x 5, in color (he began shooting transparencies in earnest in the early 1990s)[92] and black and white. He'd been published in every major rail magazine in America and had work included in more than one hundred books (his generosity to other rail authors is well known; he has always allowed them unfettered access to his archive). Magazine articles were his forte too; he authored, or provided illustration for, fifty of them. He also received the coveted Railway and Locomotive Historical Society's Fred A. and Jane R. Stindt Lifetime Achievement Award for railroad photography in 1987. This varied list of accomplishments puts him in the upper echelons of his contemporaries in terms of output and artistry; that he had worked ceaselessly is a given. The late John Szarkowski, the former curator of photography at the Museum of Modern Art, once said that "any photographer had only about seven good years of productivity in them."[93] Shaughnessy easily exceeded this dictum.

And that isn't all he did. Paralleling his avocation as a rail photographer (see fig. 33), Shaughnessy held myriad jobs throughout his life. In 1955 he started his career in the New York State Department of Transportation, became an assistant professor of civil engineering, then a consultant for a water and sewage treatment facility design and building firm, and concluded his active working life as a professional engineer and environmental health director. With all these responsibilities he still found time to be a husband, father, and devoted son. This level of loyalty, commitment, and persistence in all aspects of his life was at the heart of his achievement in train photography too.[94]

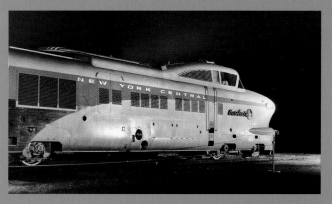

Figures 30, 31, 32, 33, and 34, clockwise:
Shaughnessy posing with copy of *Night Train*, 1961;
NYC *Aerotrain*, Albany, New York 1961; contact sheet of
builder photographs of Alco unit made by Shaughnessy,
circa mid-1970s, Colonie, New York; Shaughnessy's
business card; double-headed N de M freight train, near
Chalco, Mexico, 1961.

Figure 35

CV 2–10–4 #707
and coaling tower,
White River Junction,
Vermont, 1951

Figure 36

EL freight on the
Starrucca Viaduct,
near Lanesboro,
Pennsylvania,
1966

Figure 37

D&H PA #17 with
Laurentian along
the shore of
Lake Champlain,
New York,
1977

In the summer of 2007, as we were putting the final touches to this book, I had the opportunity to visit several Northeast settings familiar to Jim over the last half century. I wanted to stand where he had stood. One afternoon found me adjacent to the New England Central Railway (nee CV) tracks in St. Albans, Vermont, in the space the architecturally resplendent train shed once occupied—a structure that figures prominently in several Shaughnessy images (see pls. 39, 53, 89, 119, and 120) and one he even wrote an article about (see *Trains*, June 1958, pp. 56–59). Another time, I spied a bird's-eye view of the spartan roundhouse in White River Junction, Vermont. Now retrofitted, this stripped-down structure was the scene of a chance meeting between Shaughnessy and David Plowden in the summer of 1951, while both men shot CV 2–10–4 #707 near the coaling tower (see fig. 35); one wonders what the two photographers said to each other. On a weekend jaunt with close friends, I lunched at a small cafe in Island Pond, Vermont, and took a solo after-meal stroll by the train station. The depot sign still clung to the roofline, but a panting CN 4–8–2 piloting a through train to Portland, Maine, was nowhere near. I gazed across a placid Lake Champlain at the former Rutland causeway (see pl. 5) where Jim caught a peddler freight in 1956, pulled by an Alco RS3 coupled to a 2–8–2; the wooden pilings of the former low-slung trestle were gone but the sense of what had been lingered. I drove through downtown Plattsburgh, New York, and thought of the long-ago college kid watching trains from his dorm window, and swore I heard the echoing exhaust of a D&H Northern leaning into its workload, slipping on wet rail. One late afternoon, an hour before sunset, I noted the sound of my own footsteps crunching the meager ballasted remains of the abandoned D&H right-of-way beneath Starrucca Viaduct (see fig. 36). Its stone edifice gracefully sliced through the tree-dappled landscape of northeastern Pennsylvania, its arches as beautiful as ever in the crepuscular light. All were locations and landscapes Jim had explored; all were places his presence was felt.

Earlier in the year Jim and I made treks to see the Walloomsac trestles, key architectural players in those great Rutland night shots from 1961. We even decided, one snowy winter afternoon, to take a drive around downtown Troy so he could situate me spatially. I wanted to know where everything used to be—the depot, the interlocking tower, and the machine shop where his dad worked. Another time we had lunch near Johnsonville, New York, so he could show me JV tower. The former B&M relic, pitifully abandoned now and being reclaimed by nature, still stood beside a heavily trafficked Guilford ex–B&M mainline. It was easy to envision towerman R. P. Fonda on the third trick OS'ing another train through the crossovers there. On one more occasion, we rode past a bespoiled, barren landscape: the former site of the Colonie shops, now a vacant brownfield.

In retracing these steps, I came to a certain awareness: I had had the rare good fortune these past several years to keep company with a great photographer and astute historian who bore witness to perhaps the most dynamic epoch in the annals of American transportation. He photographed in a region of the country that had more railroad companies operating per square mile than any other part of the nation—many with esoteric equipment and fabled stories, both big systems and one-engine-on-the-roster wonders—and damned if he didn't cover them exhaustively, with affection and without pretense. His deep connection to this past vividly brought things into the present, helping me realize the true importance of his work—that his images are valuable documents that broaden our understanding of railroading at mid-century in a way that only thoughtful, well-conceived photographs can.

Photographs

Plate 2   Boston & Maine freight train with four GP9s crossing the Hudson River, Mechanicville, New York, 1958

Plate 3   Montpelier & Barre train with Alco S1 approaches bridge over Winooski River, Montpelier, Vermont, 1959

Plate 4 New York Central Alco S2 #8569 and cut of cars in freight yard, West Albany, New York, 1960

Plate 5 Rutland freight train with Alco RS3 #201 and 2–8–2 #32 cross Lake Champlain, Rouses Point, New York, 1951

Plate 6 Boston & Maine passenger train with E7A #3818 rolls under a covered bridge, Bath, New Hampshire, 1953

Plate 7 Canadian National 4–8–2 #6071 steams past Hamilton Junction, Ontario, 1955

Plate 8

Chicago, Burlington
& Quincy O-5-class
4–8–4 #5634
racing west toward
Galesburg, Illinois,
1956

Plate 9   Norfolk & Western Y6b 2–8–8–2 #2129 and brakeman, Boaz siding, near Vinton, Virginia, 1957

Plate 10 New York Central freight crew going to work, West Albany, New York, 1961

Plate 11

Canadian Pacific
double-headed
2–8–2s on
freight train,
Lennoxville,
Quebec,
1954

Plate 12

Canadian Pacific
engineer in
cab of 4–6–4
Royal Hudson,
Glen terminal
roundhouse,
Westmount,
Quebec,
1959

Plate 13

Baltimore & Ohio,
2–8–8–4 #7600,
on siding near
Painesville, Ohio,
1957

Plate 14 Canadian National 4–8–4 #6207 at engine terminal, Brockville, Ontario, 1958

Plate 15 Canadian Pacific double-headed freight, near Lennoxville, Quebec, 1954

Plate 18   Chicago, Burlington & Quincy 2–10–4 #6312, southern Illinois, 1956

Plate 19 Norfolk & Western workers adding water-treatment pellets to tender, Hagerstown, Maryland, 1956

Plate 20

Delaware & Hudson
Baldwin-built Shark
freight locomotive
#1216 in paint booth
at Colonie shops,
Watervliet,
New York,
1974

Plate 21

Nickel Plate
locomotive shops,
Conneaut, Ohio,
1957

Plate 22

Canadian Pacific
double-headed
2–8–2s on
freight train,
Lennoxville,
Quebec,
1956

Plate 23 Canadian Pacific freight led by two 2–8–2s crosses bridge over Pleasant River, Brownville Junction, Maine, 1955

Plate 24 Chicago, Burlington & Quincy O-5-class 4–8–4 and freight, Galesburg, Illinois, 1956

Plate 25

Driving wheels
and connecting rods
of Canadian Pacific
4–6–2 locomotive,
Three Rivers,
Quebec, 1956

Plate 26

Canadian Pacific
passenger train,
Quebec, 1955

Plate 27

Canadian National
freight train with
4–8–4 #6155,
St. Lambert, Quebec,
1957

Plate 28

Canadian National
freight with 2–8–2
pulls off Beach
subdivision, near
Burlington, Ontario,
1956

Plate 29 New Haven Railroad mechanics work on traction motor at locomotive shops, New Haven, Connecticut, 1956

Plate 30   Baltimore & Ohio fireman fills tender on 0–8–0 switch engine, Chicago, Illinois, 1956

Plate 31   Guilford Transportation freight train with ex-B&M Geep #1575, east of Mechanicville, New York, 1988

Plate 32   Norfolk & Western freight train with Y6b-class 2–8–8–4 #2179, Bonsack, Virginia, 1957

Plate 33

Troy Union Railroad
crossing guard
John Moriarity
and NYC switch
engine during
snowstorm,
Troy, New York,
1955

following spread:

Plate 34

Union Pacific
"Big Boy" 4–8–8–4
on westbound
freight train,
Dale, Wyoming,
1957

Plate 35 Canadian Pacific 4–6–4 Royal Hudson #2823, near Louisville, Quebec, 1956

Plate 36 Quebec Central, baggage man unloading packages, Vallee Junction, Quebec, 1959

Plate 41 Delaware & Hudson Alco PAs #17, #18, and #19, Colonie shops, Watervliet, New York, 1988

Plate 42   Erie Lackawanna freight train with E8 and GP7 on Starrucca Viaduct, Lanesboro, Pennsylvania, 1966

Plate 43

Boston & Maine 4–6–2 #3713,
Haverhill, Massachusetts, 1956

Plate 44 Canadian Pacific freight train and railroad crossing, eastern Quebec, 1957

Plate 45   New York Central laborer cleans number board on E8, Rensselaer, New York, 1961

Plate 46 New York Central 4–6–0 #1199, St. Thomas, Ontario, 1956

Plate 47   Troy Union Railroad trackman tightening bolt, Troy, New York, 1955

Plate 48

Boston & Maine EMDs
and outside-braced
wooden boxcars in
scrap yard, East Boston,
Massachusetts,
1968

Plate 49

Delaware & Hudson,
Baldwin Sharks
in freight yard
at Sayre,
Pennsylvania,
1975

Plate 50   New York Central Alco RS3 #8350 on the West Side High Line, New York City, 1957

Plate 51   James A. Shaughnessy, posing as station agent, Mount Holly, Vermont, 1961

Plate 52 Delaware & Hudson freight train with EL SD45 #3606 approaches Mohawk River bridge, Schenectady, New York, 1975

Plate 53   Central Vermont interior view of train shed, St. Albans, Vermont, 1956

Plate 54

Pennsylvania
coal train powered
by 2–10–0 Decapod,
Elmira Branch,
Pennsylvania,
1957

following spread:

Plate 55

Nickel Plate engineer
on 2–8–4 Berkshire
#739 awaits "highball,"
Conneaut, Ohio,
1957

Plate 56

Baltimore & Ohio
local freight train
gathering cars,
Buckhannon,
West Virginia,
1956

Plate 57

Rutland freight train with RS3
#206 on high bridge across
Walloomsac River, North Hoosick,
New York, 1959

Plate 58

Central Vermont Alco
RS3 #1859 on turntable,
Saint Albans, Vermont,
1955

Plate 59 (following spread)

Scrap yard scene of
Southern Pacific RSD5s,
Port of Albany, Albany,
New York, 1960

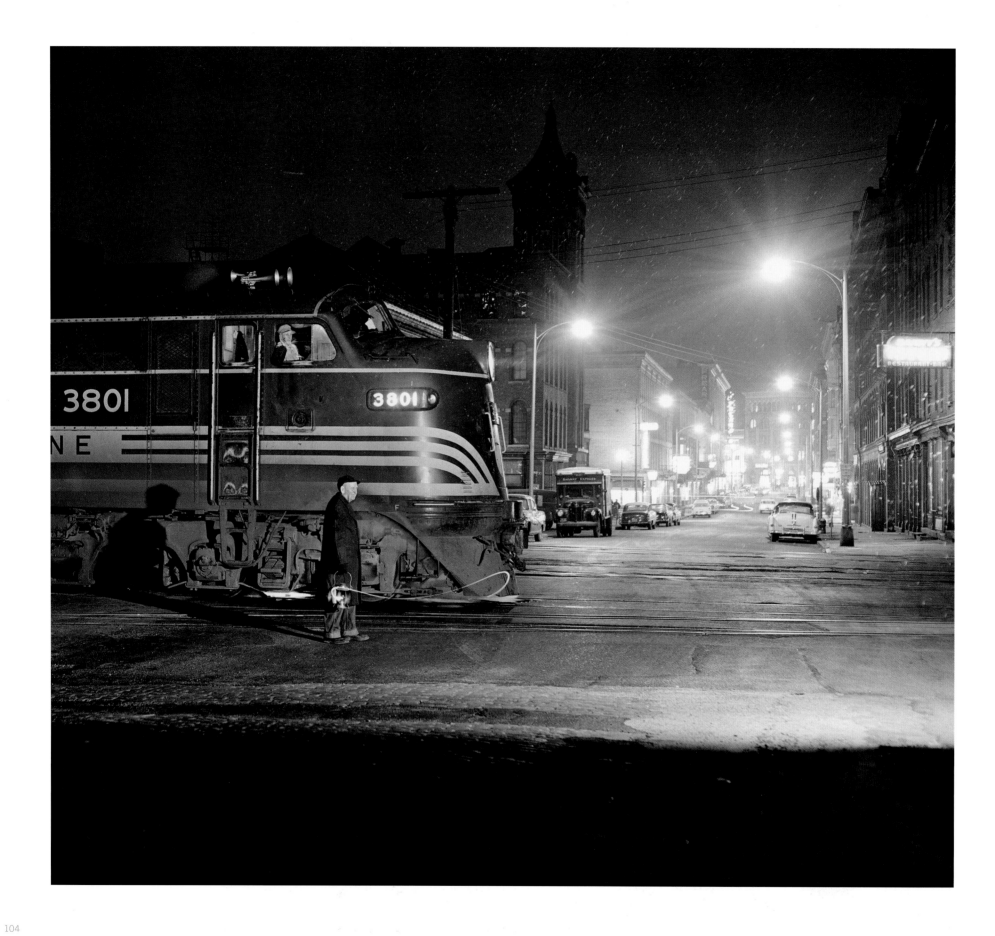

Plate 62
Wabash Railroad
freight train with F7s
#1164A and #1164,
Welland Junction,
Ontario, 1956

Plate 63
Canadian Pacific
4–6–2 #1217
outside roundhouse,
Vallee Junction,
Quebec, 1959

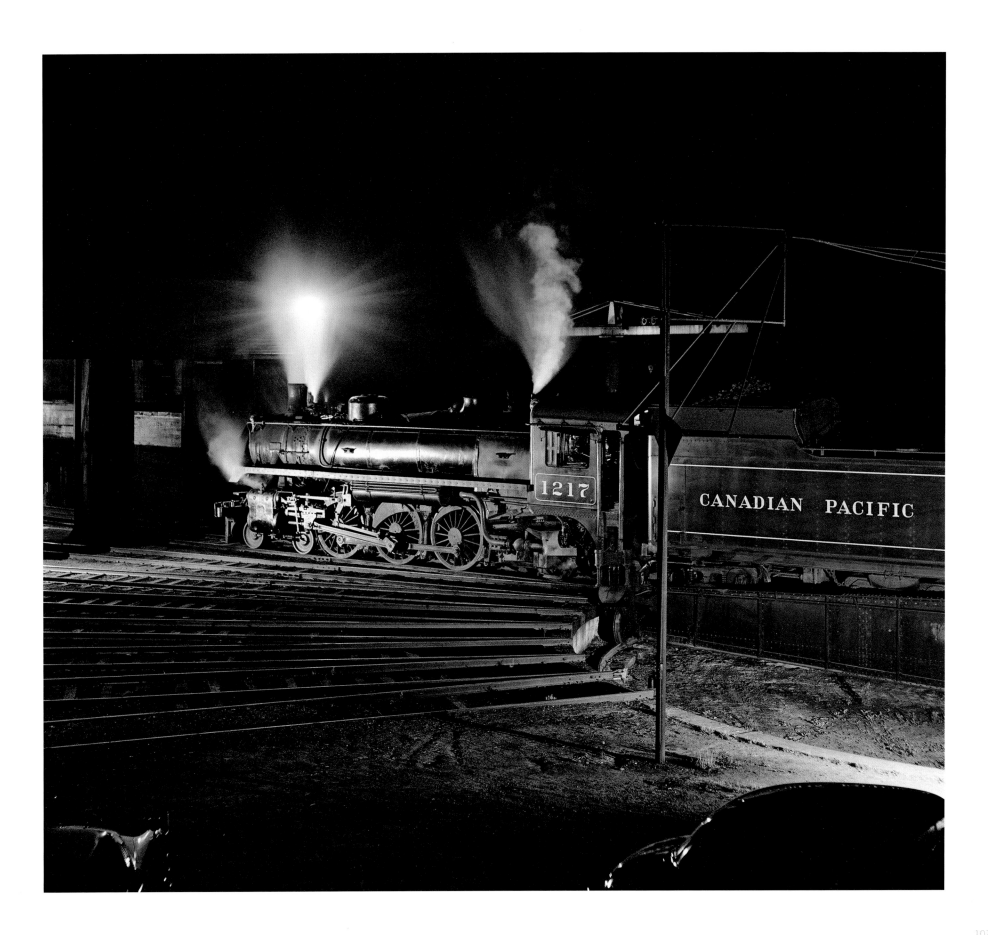

Plate 64

Central New York
Alco RS3 #101
and freight train
near East Winfield,
New York,
1988

Plate 65 Union Pacific gas-turbine #57 and freight train near Cheyenne, Wyoming, 1957

Plate 66   New York, Ontario & Western freight train with EMD FT 1350hp diesels led by #801, Kerryville, New York, 1956

Plate 67

Delaware & Hudson
brakeman and Alco PAs,
Colonie coach yard,
near Watervliet,
New York, 1976

Plate 68

New York Central
freight with Alco
FA1 #1004, east
of Chatham,
New York, 1958

Plate 71

Roundhouse laborer
replenishing sand
supply on Boston &
Maine GP9 #1726,
Mechanicville,
New York, 1958

Plate 72

Bath & Hammondsport
44-ton center cab D-1
with freight train,
Bath, New York, 1965

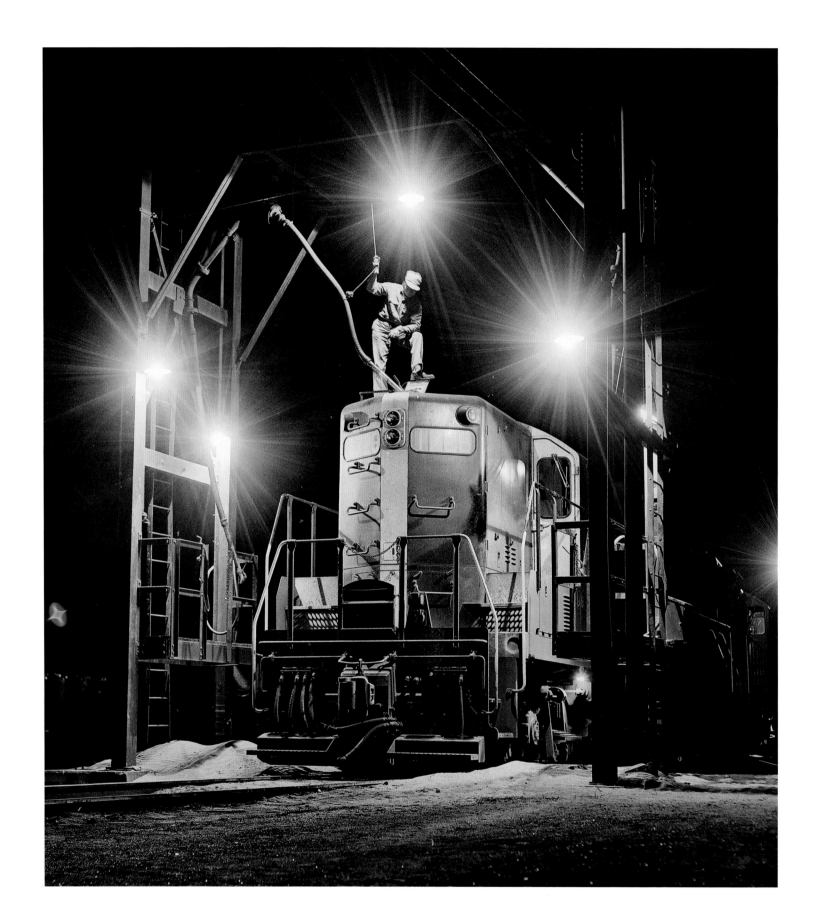

Plate 73   Norfolk & Western laborer lubricates driving rods of 4–8–2 locomotive, Hagerstown, Maryland, 1956

Plate 74   New York Central 4–6–0 #1290, St. Thomas, Ontario, 1956

Plate 75

New York Central
freight train with
Alco FA1 #1034
entering State Line
tunnel, Canaan,
New York,
1957

Plate 76

Boston & Maine,
Little Hoosac Tunnel,
North Adams,
Massachusetts,
1956

Plate 77

Canadian National
engine crew on
2–8–2 #3496,
Fort Erie, Ontario,
1956

Plate 78

Central Vermont
station agent
handing up orders,
East Northfield,
Massachusetts,
1954

Plate 79

Erie Lackawanna and
Delaware & Hudson
freight trains,
Starrucca Viaduct,
Lanesboro,
Pennsylvania,
1972

Plate 80

Boston & Maine laborer washing windows of passenger E7 #3814, Bangor, Maine, 1955

Plate 81 Norfolk & Western Y6b 2–8–8–2 #2129 and helper crew, Boaz siding, near Vinton, Virginia, 1957

Plate 82 Canadian Pacific Jubilee-type 4–4–4, #2927, Sutton, Quebec, 1955

Plate 83

Canadian Pacific
4–6–2 #2236
and engineer
Frank Bunker,
west of Galt,
Ontario, 1957

Plate 84

Baltimore & Ohio
2–8–8–4, near
Painesville, Ohio,
1955

Plate 85

Canadian National
Spadina Avenue
engine-servicing facility,
Toronto, Ontario,
1957

Plate 86

Central Vermont
0–8–0 #501 on turntable,
Brattleboro, Vermont,
1956

Plate 87   Norfolk & Western 2–8–8–2 and merchandise freight, east of Roanoke, Virginia, 1957

Plate 88 Pennsylvania station agent Louise Overhiser handing up orders to 2–10–0 #4512, Watkins Glen, New York, 1960

Plate 89
Central Vermont
station and train shed,
St. Albans, Vermont, 1956

Plate 90 Pennsylvania freight train with F7s, unknown location on Elmira Branch, Pennsylvania, 1965

Plate 91   Norfolk & Western coal train, east of Roanoke, Virginia, 1957

Plate 92   Nickel Plate train order operator prepares to hand up "flimsies," Brocton, New York, 1957

Plate 93   New York Central freight with Alco FA #1085, Pattersonville, New York, 1955

Plate 94

St. Johnsbury & Lamoille County
outside-braced wood boxcar
and covered bridge,
Swanton, Vermont, 1955

Plate 95

Canadian National
switchman and
4–6–0 #1586,
Palmerston,
Ontario,
1958

Plate 96

Pennsylvania
Railroad
and laborer
washing GG1,
Washington, DC,
1960

Plate 97

Illinois Central
hostler approaches
2–8–2 #2137,
Paducah, Kentucky,
1957

Plate 98

Denver & Rio Grande
FT #5414 and
water column,
Alamosa, Colorado,
1959

Plate 99 Pennsylvania freight train and operator handing up orders, Leolyn, Pennsylvania, 1957

Plate 100 Delaware & Hudson *Laurentian* and man with umbrella, Port Henry, New York, 1970

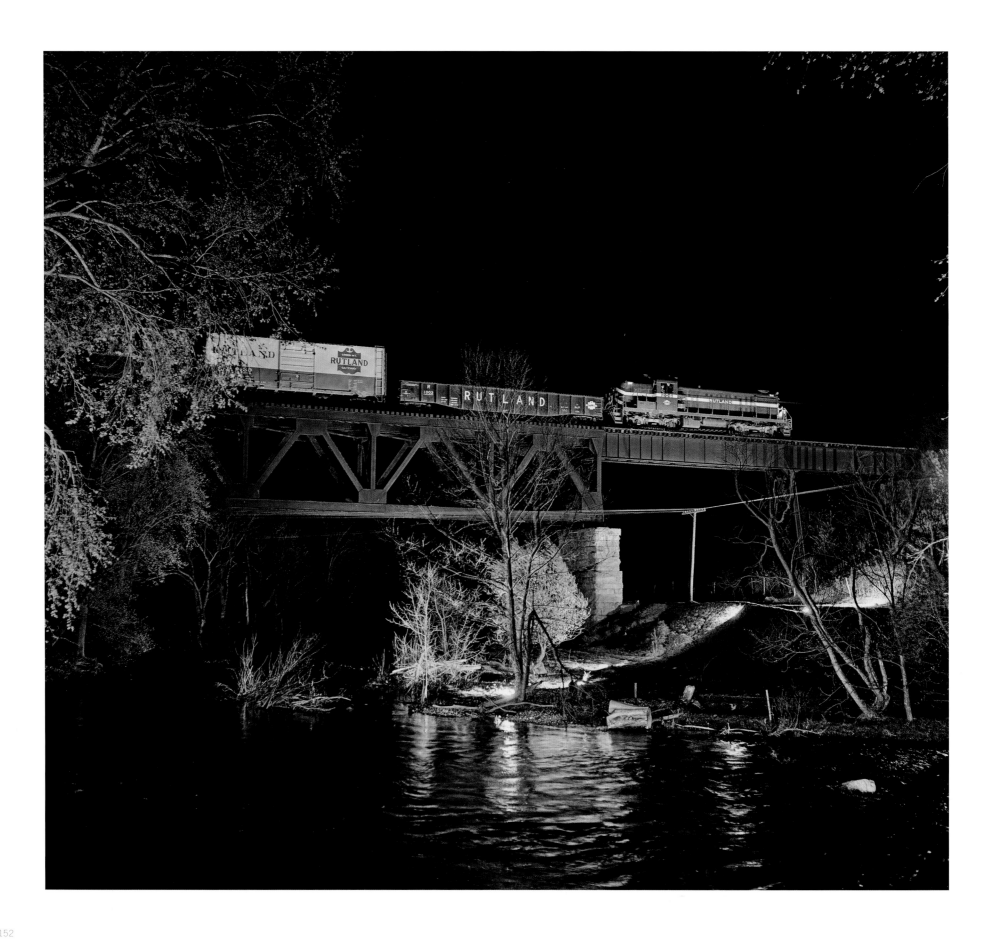

Plate 101

Rutland freight
train RC-2 with
RS3 #208 on bridge
over Walloomsac River,
near state line, New York,
1959

Plate 102

Pennsylvania freight
train with 2–10–0
#4587 and operator
handing up orders,
Elmira, New York,
1957

Plate 103

Canadian National
4–8–4 getting its
tender filled,
Turcot engine terminal,
Montreal, Quebec,
1954

Plate 104

Reading 4–8–4
with freight train
exiting off of
Rockville Bridge,
Harrisburg,
Pennsylvania,
1956

Plate 105

Grand Trunk
2–8–2 #3709
and freight train,
Sherbrooke,
Quebec,
1957

Plate 106

Canadian Pacific
2–8–0 #3488
switch engine,
St. Luc yard,
Montreal,
Quebec, 1956

Plate 107

Baltimore & Ohio
coal train crosses
Nickel Plate
mainline,
Painesville,
Ohio, 1955

Plate 108 Union Pacific freight train with "Big Boy" #4009 crosses east side of continental divide, Dale Junction, Wyoming, 1957

Plate 109 Canadian Pacific double-headed 2–8–2s on freight train, Cookshire, Quebec, 1956

Plate 110 Canadian National local passenger train #175 with 4–6–0 #1564 prepares to depart Palmerston, Ontario, 1958

Plate 112 New Haven *Patriot* powered by Alco PAs crosses Canton Viaduct, Canton, Massachusetts, 1958

Plate 113   New York Central passenger train, Castleton, New York, 1956

Plate 114 Canadian National passenger train behind 4–8–4 #6223, Welland Junction, Ontario, 1957

Plate 115 Canadian Pacific 2–8–2 #5396 and freight train in snowstorm, Lennoxville, Quebec, 1954

Plate 116

Denver & Rio Grande
freight with 2–8–2 #487,
Romeo, Colorado,
1959

Plate 117   St. Johnsbury & Lamoille County mixed train #44, Lamoille Valley, Vermont, 1955

Plate 118 St. Johnsbury & Lake Champlain freight piloted by 70-ton GE diesels #46 and #48, Wolcott, Vermont, 1967

Plate 119

Central Vermont
train shed
demolition,
St. Albans,
Vermont,
1963

Plate 120

Canadian National
4–8–4 #6173
emerging from
the train shed
at St. Albans,
Vermont,
1956

Plate 121 Baltimore & Ohio 2–8–8–4 #7611 and freight train, Failes Spur, Ohio, 1955

Plate 123 Boston & Maine 4–6–2 #3705 with southbound *Green Mountain Flyer*, North Bennington, Vermont, 1952

Plate 124   Rutland brakeman and freight train, with RS3 #202 waiting on siding, Vergennes, Vermont, 1955

Plate 125

Canadian Pacific 4–6–2 #1257
and local passenger train #40,
Sherbrooke, Quebec, 1957

Plate 127 Union Pacific freight train piloted by 4–8–4 #800, eastern Nebraska, 1955

Plate 128   St. Johnsbury & Lamoille County GE 70-ton diesels #55 and #46 with freight train, Morrisville, Vermont, 1967

Plate 129 New York Central freight and six Alcos led by FA #1042, Voorheesville, New York, 1962

Plate 130

Boston & Maine freight MB-6
at the east end of yard complex,
Mechanicville, New York, 1960

Plate 131
Chicago, Burlington
& Quincy 4–8–4
#5634 starts train
in interchange yard
at Zearing, Illinois,
1956

Plate 132
Delaware & Hudson
freight train WR-1
with caboose,
Ballston Spa,
New York,
1959

Plate 133 New York, Ontario & Western station agent, Campbell Hall, New York, 1956

Plate 135 Delaware & Hudson 4–6–6–4 on freight train (symbol AB-4) in Watervliet, New York, 1950

Plate 136   Denver & Rio Grande Mikado 2–8–2 #483, Chama, New Mexico, 1958

Plate 137

Canadian National
2–8–0 #2381
and Wabash
EMD F7A #1160
at engine terminal,
Fort Erie, Ontario,
1955

Plate 138

Delaware & Hudson
engineer boards
GE-built U23B #2318,
Mechanicville,
New York,
1975

Plate 139

New York Central local freight
with RS3 #8278 and baggage cart,
Tupper Lake, New York, 1958

Plate 140

Pennsylvania 2–10–0
and 100-car coal train,
along State Highway 14,
Ralston, Pennsylvania, 1957

Plate 141

New York Central
Laurentian, and
observation car,
Troy Union Station,
Troy, New York,
1955

following spread:

Plate 142

Two Nickel Plate
workers and 2–8–4
Berkshire #731
and sister locomotive
in roundhouse,
Conneaut, Ohio,
1957

Afterword & Captions

Looking Back: Sixty Years of Railroad Photography   Jim Shaughnessy

During almost six decades of photographing railroads I have had many memorable experiences. Reviewing my many images, a fraction of which are offered in this volume, brought to mind some of those wonderful occasions and served as a reminder that I gained more in this quest than just a photographic record of times past.

In my early teens, before I owned a car or could even drive one, my parents indulged my passion. Frequently Sunday drives in the country would end at, or be specifically directed toward, a railroad point of interest. Even before I began serious photography, I was interested in trains (as well as tugboats, airplanes, and other mechanized things). These family activities encouraged the interest and knowledge that would carry me through the rest of my life, professionally and avocationally.

On one such occasion, in the late 1940s, we stopped at the Delaware & Hudson's roundhouse in Whitehall, New York. In those days, following World War II, most railroad personnel were quite cordial and seemed to appreciate someone, especially a kid, who was interested in what they did. My patient mother sat in the car while my father and I explored. The time passed slowly for my mother, but after a while a big Northern-type 4–8–4 steam locomotive slowly passed where the car was parked. To her astonishment, I was at the throttle. My father and I had met a wonderful gentleman—Henry Stewart, the engine hostler on duty at the time—and he invited us to ride around the terminal with him in the locomotive cab as he moved it from one servicing point to another, finally spotting it on the ready track. I was running the 4–8–4 but Henry was standing right behind me.

Interestingly, a decade later, in June 1957, writer friend Roderick Craib and I arranged to spend part of a day with Henry to compile an illustrated story of a typical day at his hostler job. I began by photographing him leaving his house in the morning and arriving at the roundhouse in his two-door black Studebaker sedan. We continued to record his various activities, in word and image, as he moved diesels around the terminal to be fueled, added sand for traction, cleaned the cab windows, iced the crew's water cooler, and eased units in and out of the shop area for running repairs. His final move for a set of locomotives would be to spot them on the ready track for the next outbound crew to board. The story, unfortunately, was never published, but the project, along with the steam cab experience ten years earlier, established a long-lasting friendship.

My kindred-spirit friend John Pickett and I decided to go to Colorado in late September 1959 and ride on the Rio Grande narrow-gauge railway over Cumbres Pass sponsored by the Kiwanis Club of Alamosa, Colorado. We departed New York City on a TWA Super Constellation (he on his company pass and me for a $78 coach ticket), and changed at Denver to a vintage Frontier Airlines DC-3 to Alamosa. We arrived several days before the excursion to rent a car and do some freight train photography on the line running over Cumbres Pass to Chama, New Mexico. This plan worked well, netting us some pacing shots along the three-rail section paralleling the highway south of Alamosa toward Antonito and a nice selection of spectacular double-header action out of Chama yard to the summit of Cumbres Pass.

The freight train traffic was sporadic at the time, with a train only running one way on a given day, or in some cases none at all. One morning we followed a double-headed freight east out of Chama, up the stiff grade to the summit of the pass, capturing some of the wonderful scenes that these trains always provide. At the summit, while the train crew was cutting off the second locomotive and doing some switching, a violent hail storm hit, covering the ground with sugar-like crystals. We decided not to follow the train farther east, as the little-used dirt road avoided the rail line for most of the distance to Antonito. It was getting late and there would not be a chance for more photography that day. We then discovered that when the car was moving in reverse the odometer turned backwards, and having nothing else to do we backed all the way down the mostly deserted road to Chama, canceling all the miles we had put on the rented car that morning.

To return to Alamosa the next day we chose to go via Wolf Creek Pass, but as we approached it from the west we found the Highway Patrol had closed the road to any vehicle without tire chains because of an early blizzard. We backtracked and purchased chains for the rental car, put 400 pounds of rocks in the trunk for traction, and headed for the hill, passing stalled tractor-trailers, cars in ditches, and occasional flashes of lightning. We even stopped to take some photos and then effortlessly continued up the grade—going forward this time.

When the time came for the Kiwanis Club special to run west out of Alamosa that weekend, the weather had deteriorated to the point that snow was blocking the railroad over Cumbres Pass—and the trip was canceled.

Storms were always a potential problem on winter trips to Quebec's Eastern Townships. But the journey was always rewarding, as the Canadian Pacific's railroad from Montreal to Saint John, New Brunswick, had more than a 700 percent increase in traffic when the St. Lawrence River froze over. To move these heavy trains of prairie grain over this hilly route required that each train be hauled by double-headed steam locomotives. The train would meet another similarly powered train, coming in the opposite direction, at almost every small town with a passing track on the route.

Longtime friend Sandy Worthen would drive out from Montreal, where he worked, and meet me in Ayres Cliff, about twenty miles north of the U.S. border from Newport, Vermont. He had grown up in Ayres Cliff, and his elderly mother still lived in the family home. From this base of operations we would take day trips to shoot the double-headed trains running through Sherbrooke and the surrounding area, as well as the Canadian National activity on the line up from Portland, Maine, to Montreal. The Quebec Central, a Canadian Pacific subsidiary, also ran two passenger trains and some freight between Quebec City and Sherbrooke using vintage CP locomotives and equipment.

Snow is a necessary ingredient for great winter pictures, and it was usually in abundance, but sometimes it could be more a problem than an asset. On one visit in 1956 it started to snow on Saturday afternoon and continued through the night. By noon Sunday my car was heavily covered in the driveway of Sandy's mother's house in Ayres Cliff. After clearing it off I headed south on Route 5 toward the Vermont border at Newport. There was a high ridge between me and the border called Duffern Heights, where the embankments on either side of the road would encourage blowing snow to drift between them—and it did!

I made a run at the two rapidly filling ruts in what looked like the road and after much wheel spinning and fishtailing, I finally made it through the cut to a flat but snow-covered road that took me the remaining distance to the border. My troubles, however, weren't over. Vermont Route 100, between Newport and Troy, headed directly west into the driving snow, and it turned into a whiteout. I kept the car on the road by looking for mailboxes and fenceposts on either side. Suddenly I saw an oncoming car about 25 feet ahead of me. Fortunately we were on slightly different courses and had enough room between us to avoid a collision. The car immediately disappeared in my rearview mirror. The remainder of the route to Burlington was in sheltered valleys, and despite six inches of snow on the road the going became almost pleasant.

Sandy later told me that he had made it only a few miles west to Magog in his attempt to return to Montreal that afternoon, and had to return to Ayres Cliff, where he was marooned for two days. No cars had made it over Duffern Heights until the following Wednesday.

The driving was much easier on a weekend visit with John Pickett to Virginia's Shenandoah Valley in August 1956. I drove to Philadelphia, where John was working for United Airlines, and we departed Saturday morning in his 1955 Ford. Luckily, we caught a Reading Railroad 4–8–4 west of Harrisburg, coming off the famous Rockville stone arch bridge spanning the Susquehanna River, before we turned south

toward Hagerstown and Norfolk & Western territory. The locomotive was one of several that had been leased by the Pennsylvania to get them through a traffic surge. After taking some photos at the big bridge across the Potomac River, near the Civil War battlefield of Antietam—one of which I blew by not removing the dark slide from my 4 x 5 film holder before releasing the shutter and uttered an expletive that could probably have been heard as far down the river as Washington, DC—we followed a N&W 2–8–8–2 Y6b down the Shenandoah Valley line. There were a number of stretches where the railroad paralleled U.S. Route 11. John thought it was a great opportunity to take some pacing shots from the car as we moved at the same speed as the train. He stopped the car and got in the back seat so he could be completely free to handle his camera, and I took the wheel. Soon we were barreling along beside the big roaring machine and it was indeed a sight to behold—and to photograph. In between shots John looked up and, to his horror, I was shooting photos too—keeping his car on course by holding my knees against the steering wheel. It was a great opportunity!

These reminiscences are but a few of the many wonderful experiences I have had in my lifelong quest to capture the railroads on film. It would take another book to recount the people I have met, the places I have been, the other wonders of the world I have seen, and the great personal satisfaction I have attained in my quest. In every expedition I made, whether it was to nearby Mechanicville yard, to remote villages in central Mexico, through the winter snows of Canada, into the high mountains of the American West, or in seventeen countries of Europe, there was always something new to see and learn from the railroads themselves and beyond. Compiling the illustrations for this volume has allowed me to make some of those wonderful journeys once more.

Jim Shaughnessy
Troy, New York
February 2008

Figure 38
Denver & Rio Grande
Mikado 2–8–2 #488
with cattle extra,
La Jara, Colorado,
1963

Figure 1 Engineer of Canadian National 4–6–2 #5288 leans out cab window, Bromptonville, Quebec, February 24, 1957

The engineer of Canadian National 4–6–2 #5288, leading the morning passenger train from Sherbrooke, Quebec, to Montreal down the St. Francis River valley, leans out into the –20°F breeze as he rolls north at 60 mph. This type of image, which brings the viewer into the photographer's experience, was inspired by the immediacy of the photojournalistic style that emerged in the 1930s. Shaughnessy, being naturally curious and open to experimentation, appropriated various techniques like this for his rail photography.

Figure 2 Boston & Maine passenger train with E7 #3812, Troy Union Station, Troy, New York, 1958

An overnight passenger and mail train from Boston arrives at the Troy Union Station while the downtown area, along Sixth Avenue, digs out from an overnight snowfall. Troy's Union Station went through many incarnations. The last, shown here, was erected in 1900 and designed by the architectural firm of Reed and Stem. It featured Beaux Arts columns and umbrella platforms. In 1910 the station hosted 130 passenger trains daily. It was demolished in 1958 during an era of urban renewal—sadly, before the historic building preservation movement had begun.

Figure 9 Delaware & Hudson 4–8–4 #301 and freight train, Plattsburgh, New York, February 10, 1952

The Delaware & Hudson stabled an impressive roster of steam locomotives during its long existence, especially at the end of the steam era. Here 4–8–4 Northern-type #301 with smoke lifters (affectionately known as "elephant ears") struggles to get a southbound freight, carrying Canadian newsprint paper, moving after making a pickup in Plattsburgh, New York, on the shore of Lake Champlain, where the photographer spent a year going to college in 1951–52.

Figure 26 Wabash F7A #1160 and CN 2–8–2 #3431, Fort Erie, Ontario, September 22, 1956

A quiet night in Fort Erie, Ontario, finds Wabash F7A #1150 and CN 2–8–2 #3431 resting in the CN engine terminal. The Wabash railroad operated with trackage rights on the CN line across southern Ontario from Windsor, where it ran freight but no passenger trains. One of Shaughnessy's early influences was the portraiture of the Canadian photographer Josuf Karsh, who utilized the kind of dramatic lighting in his images seen here. Shaughnessy routinely made open-air studios out of engine servicing areas, creating locomotive portraits that became a defining component of his style.

Figure 27 Portrait of Delaware & Hudson engineer Henry Stewart inside cab of Alco RS3, Whitehall, New York, 1957

Engineer Henry Stewart is the terminal hostler (the engineman who moves the locomotives around to the various servicing points in the engine terminal) in the D&H Whitehall, New York, yard. This shot was part of a day-in-the-life story Shaughnessy did on Stewart in 1957.

Figure 28 Derailment of Rutland *Mount Royal* passenger train, Arlington, Vermont, April 1949

The Rutland's New York to Montreal overnight train through western Vermont was named the *Mount Royal*. In April 1949 it derailed south of Arlington, Vermont, after spring floods undermined the roadbed when a drain pipe plugged, causing a washout. In the distance a steam-powered Big Hook wrecking crane is about to start lifting the passenger cars back onto the track. No passengers were seriously injured.

Figure 29 New York, Ontario & Western brakeman and NW2 #122 in freight yard, Middletown, New York, 1957

A brakeman sets the hand brake on a boxcar spotted in the NYO&W's yard in Middletown, New York, as NW2 #122 waits patiently. This image was made a few weeks before the railroad abandoned all of its lines, as bankruptcy was declared due to changing transportation patterns in its service area. In its day the NYO&W hauled milk, farm products, coal, and passengers, but in the end there was not enough lineside business to keep it solvent.

Plate 1 Denver & Rio Grande roundhouse, machinists and Mikado 2–8–2 #473, Alamosa, Colorado, September 1, 1959

Two Rio Grande machinists ponder the next move needed to keep three-foot-gauge Mikado 2–8–2 #473 on the road after she departs the solitude of the Alamosa, Colorado, roundhouse. Steam locomotion required the skills of many crafts: boilermakers, plumbers, electricians, laborers, and welders, to say nothing of firemen and engineers. In more rural settings oftentimes railroaders had to wear several hats, or fabricate parts, to keep the equipment running.

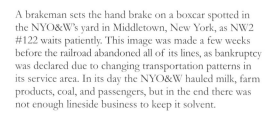

Plate 2 Boston & Maine freight train with four GP9s crossing the Hudson River, Mechanicville, New York, 1958

Four EMD GP9 units apply all their 7000 hp to a New England–bound freight train; the train, and the deck truss bridge it's on, are mirrored in the placid water of the Hudson River at Mechanicville, New York. Most of the freight traffic to northern Massachusetts and upper New England took this route.

Plate 3 Montpelier & Barre train with Alco S1 approaches bridge over Winooski River, Montpelier, Vermont, 1959

A Montpelier & Barre freight with ex-B&M Alco S1-type 600hp yard switcher approaches the bridge over the Winooski River in Montpelier, Vermont. This portion of the M&B was once a CV branch line that ran from Montpelier to Barre and on through to Williamstown, Vermont, where it ended. In the mid-1960s it was sold to short line operator Sam Pinsley.

Plate 4 New York Central Alco S2 #8569 and cut of cars in freight yard, West Albany, New York, November 18, 1960

A carload of Studebaker automobiles waits to be spotted by Alco S2 switch engine #8569 at the unloading ramp in the New York Central's West Albany yard.

Plate 5 Rutland freight train with Alco RS3 #201 and 2-8-2 #32 cross Lake Champlain, Rouses Point, New York, 1951

A new Alco RS3 #201 diesel helps Rutland veteran 2-8-2 #32 across the north end of Lake Champlain at Rouses Point, New York, on a creaking wooden trestle, as they make their way across the top of New York state to a connection with the NYC at Malone Junction, New York.

Plate 6 Boston & Maine passenger train with E7A #3818 rolls under a covered bridge, Bath, New Hampshire, 1953

In a classic New England setting, a Boston & Maine local passenger train from Berlin, New Hampshire, to White River Junction, Vermont, rolls under a covered bridge over the Gale River at Bath, New Hampshire. Covered bridges came into existence because their structural elements needed protection from the ravages of inclement Northeastern weather. In this classic New England tableau, Shaughnessy shows the defining characteristic of his rail photography: contextualization of the railroad and its surrounding environment, in this case rural, small-town America.

Plate 7 Canadian National 4-8-2 #6071 steams past Hamilton Junction, Ontario, February 4, 1955

A cold but sunny day greets a Toronto-bound passenger train from Hamilton at Hamilton Junction control tower on the Canadian National line. This train, hauled by one of twenty bullet-nose Mountain-type locomotives on the CN's roster, had originated in Windsor and was required to make a reverse move for several miles to reach downtown Hamilton, which was not located on the direct east-west mainline of CN's southern Ontario track network. It is seen returning along the shore of Lake Ontario to rejoin the main route and continue its journey to Toronto.

Plate 8 Chicago, Burlington & Quincy O-5-class 4-8-4 #5634 racing west toward Galesburg, Illinois, November 24, 1956

The thundering mass of a CB&Q O-5-class 4-8-4 #5634 races west toward Galesburg, Illinois, along U.S. Highway 34 on an overcast afternoon. This was the last stand for Burlington's great steam locomotives. A record wheat harvest across the prairies the previous summer required the reactivation of stored steam engines, smartly set aside by the company's management for emergency service, even as new GP9s arrived on the property. Photographer John Pickett accompanied Shaughnessy on this trip to the Midwest, helping with the driving, which allowed for unique action shots. With his numerous pacing images, Jim wanted to capture the sensation of movement—and the moment he had while riding in a car chasing a train at speed.

Plate 9 Norfolk & Western Y6b 2-8-8-2 #2129 and brakeman, Boaz siding, near Vinton, Virginia, August 6, 1957

The brakeman of massive Norfolk & Western Y6b 2-8-8-2 #2129 stands by the pilot beam of the helper engine on a side track at Boaz, near Vinton, Virginia, several miles west of Roanoke, waiting for a heavy 15,000-ton eastbound coal train that will need help ascending the significant slopes of Blue Ridge grade.

Plate 10 New York Central freight crew going to work, West Albany, New York, February 22, 1961

The evening switching crew at New York Central's West Albany freight yard board their caboose and prepare for the night's switching duties. This yard was a busy classification point until the NYC created the Castleton cutoff and opened the Selkirk yards in 1924, effectively bypassing the congestion often caused by West Albany Hill, and the helper service required to lift trains over it. The yard was relegated to serving local customers. Adjacent to it were the West Albany shops, a giant complex that was the principal maintenance base for all NYC lines east of Buffalo; it included a steam locomotive facility. With the arrival of diesels the vast West Albany shop complex was abandoned and was completely razed by spring 1966.

Plate 11 Canadian Pacific double-headed 2-8-2s on freight train, Lennoxville, Quebec, January 29, 1954

A clear crisp winter's day finds one of the frequent Canadian Pacific double-headed freight trains on the Montreal-to-St. John, New Brunswick, line across southern Quebec leaving Lennoxville and about to cross the frozen St. Francis River. The −20°F temperature turns the exhaust steam from the two 2-8-2s into a towering cloud and will mark their passage through the rolling countryside just north of Vermont. Winters saw a vast increase in traffic on this route to the ice-free port when the St. Lawrence River around Montreal froze over for the season.

Plate 12 Canadian Pacific engineer in cab of 4-6-4 Royal Hudson, Glen terminal roundhouse, Westmount, Quebec, 1959

A Canadian Pacific engineer looks back from the cab of his Royal Hudson for a signal to move his 4-6-4 onto the turntable at the Glen terminal roundhouse in Westmount, Quebec. Located three miles from Montreal's Windsor Station, Glen terminal was the primary servicing facility for CP's passenger locomotives and cars departing on trains from that station. The Montreal Locomotive Works delivered the first Hudsons to the CP in 1929. Later, streamlined versions of the engines, often considered the most beautiful locomotives in the world, were delivered between 1937 and 1939. Representing some of the last great modern steam technology on the railway, these engines were usually assigned the highest-profile passenger service roles on transcontinental trains.

Plate 13 Baltimore & Ohio, 2-8-8-4 #7600, on siding near Painesville, Ohio, 1957

B&O's 2-8-8-4s were the last "new" steam engines the company ordered from Baldwin in 1944–45. Originally assigned to the mountainous Cumberland and Pittsburgh divisions they ended their days in the coal regions of Ohio.

Plate 14 Canadian National 4-8-4 #6207 at engine terminal, Brockville, Ontario, August 23, 1958

Canadian National 4-8-4 #6207 is highlighted by the headlight beam of a companion locomotive on an adjacent track in the servicing area of the Brockville, Ontario, engine terminal.

Plate 15   Canadian Pacific double-headed freight, near Lennoxville, Quebec, January 1954

A double-headed Canadian Pacific freight heads east near Lennoxville, Quebec, on the line leading to Saint John, New Brunswick. Winters saw a vast increase in traffic on this route to the ice-free port when the St. Lawrence River around Montreal froze over for the season.

Plate 16   Delaware & Hudson yardmaster Paul Mooney at Colonie yard, Watervliet, New York, February 23, 1961

Delaware & Hudson yardmaster Paul Mooney throws a turnout in the Colonie yard at Watervliet, New York, while helping assemble the consist of the Whitehall fast freight for its nightly round-trip journey north to its namesake city. The *WFF* left Colonie around 9 p.m., stopping to set out and pick up cars at Mechanicville, Saratoga, Fort Edward, and then on to Whitehall, returning over the same route and doing work as needed. Mooney was a yardmaster, as was his father before him. Shaughnessy was a friend of Mooney's and asked him to pose for the photograph. This image was so iconographic that Lucius Beebe used it in his *Central Pacific and Southern Pacific* book. There, Mooney was identified as a switchman on the Southern Pacific in the foothills of the Sierra Nevada.

Plate 17   Nickel Plate 2–8–4 #774 with freight train, Conneaut, Ohio, April 16, 1957

A Nickel Plate (New York, Chicago & St. Louis Railroad) 2–8–4 Berkshire waits in Conneaut, Ohio, to depart with a fast freight train bound for Buffalo, New York, from Chicago, Illinois. This relatively small line was a fierce competitor to the giant NYC in the traffic from the Midwest to eastern gateways via Buffalo. Cleveland's Van Sweringen brothers bought the NKP for $8.5 million on April 13, 1916. The railroad served a large area, with trackage in New York, Pennsylvania, Ohio, Indiana, and Illinois. In 1964, the Nickel Plate Road and several other midwestern carriers were merged into the Norfolk & Western Railway.

Plate 18   Chicago, Burlington & Quincy 2–10–4 #6312, southern Illinois, 1956

The Burlington's 2–10–4s were built by Baldwin Locomotive Works from 1927–35. At 504,570 pounds with 83,300 pounds of tractive effort they were the CB&Q's heaviest steam engines. With 64˝ drivers they saw freight service on coal drags originating in southern Illinois. The "Q" called its 2–10–4s the "Colorado" type, but many of the engines, ironically, never ran in the Columbine state.

Plate 19   Norfolk & Western workers adding water-treatment pellets to tender, Hagerstown, Maryland, August 21, 1956

Two terminal laborers work together to add water-treatment chemical pellets, which reduce boiler corrosion, to the huge tender of one of the N&W's massive Y6b 2–8–8–2 locomotives in Hagerstown, Maryland. This was one of the first stops that Jim Shaughnessy and John Pickett made on their foray to photograph the N&W in the summer of 1956.

Plate 20   Delaware & Hudson Baldwin-built Shark freight locomotive #1216 in paint booth at Colonie shops, Watervliet, New York, September 10, 1974

Baldwin-built Shark freight locomotive #1216 is seen here in the paint booth at D&H's Colonie shop having the "War Bonnet" paint configuration applied, which first appeared on the road's ex–Santa Fe Alco PA passenger units. This, and a companion first-generation Baldwin unit, was obtained by the D&H for excursion and other services by preservation-minded president C. B. Sterzing. The Sharks were purchased in 1978 from the D&H by John Kunzie and the Castolite Corporation, and leased for $100 a day to the Michigan & Northern for road operation. However, mechanical problems plagued them and they are now stored, inoperable, in the Escanaba and Lake Superior shops at Wells, Michigan.

Plate 21 Nickel Plate locomotive shops, Conneaut, Ohio, 1957

The shop floor for heavy locomotive repairs on the Nickel Plate at Conneaut, Ohio, is seen from the overhead crane operator's cab. NKP was one of the railroads that had a sizable fleet of newer, more efficient steamers—mainly fast and powerful 2–8–4 Berkshire-type freight locomotives—and used to successfully compete with neighbor NYC between Buffalo, New York, and Chicago, Illinois. The NKP workforce was fully committed to maintaining them till the end of steam operations, which lasted here much longer than on many other U.S. railroads—as this busy scene shows.

Plate 22   Canadian Pacific double-headed 2–8–2s on freight train, Lennoxville, Quebec, January, 1956

The volume of traffic on Canadian Pacific's route between Montreal and Saint John, New Brunswick, increased dramatically during the winter months, when the St. Lawrence River froze. This rail route was located at right angles to many river valleys in eastern Quebec and the state of Maine, requiring two locomotives on almost every freight train to deal with the grades encountered.

Plate 23   Canadian Pacific freight led by two 2–8–2s crosses bridge over Pleasant River, Brownville Junction, Maine, 1955

A Canadian Pacific freight led by two heavy 2–8–2s crosses the bridge over the Pleasant River at Brownville Junction, Maine, a division and crew change point, en route to tidewater at Saint John, New Brunswick. This rail line crossed the Pine Tree State on a CP subsidiary called the International of Maine, which opened in 1889.

Plate 24   Chicago, Burlington & Quincy O-5-class 4–8–4 and freight, Galesburg, Illinois, November 25, 1956

One of the last Burlington steam locomotives to operate in regular service dramatically departs from Galesburg, Illinois, with a long train of wheat bound for Great Lakes ports. The CB&Q's O-5 class were built at the railroad's West Burlington shops. These engines were extremely excellent examples of the most modern dual-service steam locomotive used by the CB&Q on its Chicago–Twin Cities and Chicago–Omaha–Denver mainlines.

Plate 25   Driving wheels and connecting rods of Canadian Pacific 4–6–2 locomotive, Three Rivers, Quebec, 1956

A Canadian Pacific 4–6–2 Pacific-type basks in the rays of sunlight streaming through the roundhouse windows. Shaughnessy enjoyed this close proximity to locomotives. For him a steam locomotive was truly a "thing of beauty, power and purpose."

Plate 26   Canadian Pacific passenger train, Quebec, 1955

A Montreal-bound CP passenger train from the Maritime Provinces streaks across a bridge at Eastman, Quebec, shortly after dawn on a cold Canadian morning.

Plate 27   Canadian National freight train with 4–8–4 #6155, St. Lambert, Quebec, November 9, 1957

A Canadian National freight train approaches a grade crossing east of St. Lambert, Quebec, in the French-speaking area of Canada, which requires bilingual railroad crossing protection, as shown by this rare "wig-wag" signal in French. The "x" sign shape is universal. This route traversed the Victoria Bridge, the first to cross the St. Lawrence River. Erected in 1859, it was of tubular-type construction made from huge solid iron plate.

Plate 28   Canadian National freight with 2–8–2 pulls off Beach subdivision, near Burlington, Ontario, August 18, 1956

Seen from the crossing tender's perch at Brant Street in Burlington, Ontario, on a rainy summer day, a 2–8–2 Mikado-powered freight train on the Beach subdivision approaches the junction with the Oakville sub mainline as a Ford station wagon crosses ahead of the lowering gates. The Beach sub provided a 7.8-mile short cut bypassing Hamilton and the busy terminal trackage of Canada's steel city. The photographer's location, within the crossing tender, provided protection from the wet weather and a unique means of framing the composition.

Plate 29   New Haven Railroad mechanics work on traction motor at locomotive shops, New Haven, Connecticut, July 14, 1956

Mechanics work on a traction motor removed from one of the fleet of EMD FL9s in the New Haven's shop complex in its namesake city. In electrified territory the FL9 locomotive could draw power from under-running third rail by means of retractable shoes operated by pneumatic cylinders. The New Haven was the pioneer of heavy mainline railroad electrification in the United States. Early plans to extend the catenary to Boston were never completed due to the NH's perennial financial problems.

Plate 30   Baltimore & Ohio fireman fills tender on 0–8–0 switch engine, Chicago, Illinois, 1956

The fireman on a B&O 0–8–0 switch engine fills the tender to overflowing at the engine terminal in Chicago, Illinois. The tender on this switch engine held approximately 10,000 gallons, the usual amount consumed, depending on workload, during one eight-hour shift shunting freight cars in the yards.

Plate 31   Guilford Transportation freight train with ex–B&M Geep #1575, east of Mechanicville, New York, January, 1988

In a picture-postcard setting only a wintry New England day can afford, a local Guilford Transportation freight with ex–B&M Geep #1575, eases through a snowy setting at Snyder's on the Boston & Maine's tracks five miles east of Mechanicville, New York. The D&H, and now the CP, have trackage rights agreements over this line to reach the south end of the former D&H Washington Branch at Eagle Bridge, now the Batten Kill Railroad. Shaughnessy frequented this location, which was a ten-minute drive from his home in Troy.

Plate 32   Norfolk & Western freight train with Y6b-class 2–8–8–4 #2179, Bonsack, Virginia, 1957

Norfolk & Western freight train with Y6b-class 2–8–8–4 #2179 approaches the top of the hill at Bonsack, Virginia, about three miles west of Blue Ridge Station. The fireman concentrates on fueling the giant locomtotive as it battles gravity hauling a 150-car coal train up the west side of the Blue Ridge Mountains east of Roanoke, Virginia.

Plate 33   Troy Union Railroad crossing guard John Moriarity and NYC switch engine during snowstorm, Troy, New York, March 1955

Troy Union Railroad crossing guard John Moriarity endures a heavy snowfall in the middle of the Broadway street crossing at the south end of the Union Station, while an NYC Alco switch engine on track #1 places baggage cars to be loaded at the express section of the facility. Due to constant train and switching movements live flagmen, rather than gates, always guarded the two crossings at Broadway and Fulton Street, which were at either end of the station platforms and only a city block apart. This image ran on the front cover of the *Trains* December issue in 1956.

Plate 34   Union Pacific "Big Boy" 4–8–8–4 on westbound freight train, Dale, Wyoming, August 20, 1957

Even a Union Pacific "Big Boy," the largest steam locomotive ever built, is dwarfed by the Wyoming high country of Sherman Hill, on the continental divide between Cheyenne and Laramie. This westbound freight is running on the new line, built after World War II, which was designed to ease stiff westbound gradients.

Plate 35   Canadian Pacific 4–6–4 Royal Hudson #2823, near Louisville, Quebec, November 10, 1956

Canadian Pacific Royal Hudson 4–6–4 #2823 roars down the north shore of the St. Lawrence near Louisville, Quebec, at 90 miph, 20 miles west of Three Rivers, with a passenger train from Montreal. Friend Sandy Worthen was driving his new 1956 two-tone Oldsmobile along the paralleling highway at 85 mph; even at that speed the Royal Hudson left the two photographers behind. Worthen, also a photographer, shot Kodachrome slides instead of black and white because he didn't have darkroom capability and thought color would be more important in the future. Shaughnessy would not transition to shooting color full-time until the early 1990s.

Plate 36   Quebec Central, baggage man unloading packages, Vallee Junction, Quebec, May 30, 1959

A French-Canadian baggage man, clad in white shirt, tie, and suspenders, unloads mail and express from an impeccably maintained wooden CP combination car used on the daily mixed train from Lac Frontiere at Vallee Junction, Quebec. The Quebec Central Railway was a subsidiary of the Canadian Pacific, and most of the equipment used on the line was leased from the parent company.

Plate 37   National Railways of Mexico freight train and 2–8–0 #263 departs Chalco, Mexico, March 16, 1961

A local narrow-gauge Ne de M freight train with oil burning 2–8–0 #263 on the headend departs Chalco, a town 35 kilometers south of Mexico City on the 137-kilometer line to Cuautla.

Plate 38   Nickel Plate freight train and 2–8–4, Dunkirk, New York, March 16, 1957

A westbound Nickel Plate freight led by one of its powerful 2–8–4 Berkshires has a wheel on a Buffalo-to-Chicago consist near Dunkirk, New York. The NKP prided itself in its ability to move traffic faster and more reliably on its single-track line than neighboring giant NYC could in the Chicago-to-East Coast market. The three-quarter wedge aesthetic became the default style employed by most railfan photographers before 1940. Shaughnessy never consciously adopted it, although he wasn't opposed to it and would sometimes make a wedge shot "for the record if the light were right."

Plate 39   Canadian National 4–8–4 #6208 with the *Washingtonian*, St. Albans, Vermont, December 26, 1955

On the day after Christmas, the overnight train between Montreal, Quebec, and Washington, DC—the *Washingtonian* —is framed in a train shed portal at CV's St. Albans station. CN 4–8–4 #6208 will hustle the sleeping passengers over the subtle spine of the Green Mountains to White River Junction, where other railroads, like the B&M, New Haven, and PRR (in New York City) will forward them to Washington. When the locomotive stopped, Shaughnessy had ten minutes to make pictures during the crew change (from CN to CV personnel). For this image, which is about a sixty-second time exposure, Jim opened his shutter, stayed out of the camera's field of view, and walked around firing #5 and #25 flashbulbs to illuminate the locomotive and main station building behind the 4–8–4 engine.

Plate 40   Delaware & Hudson's Colonie shops, near Watervliet, New York, April 21, 1971

Two sets of passenger train power await assignment inside D&H's shops at Colonie, near Watervliet, New York. Two of the D&H's famous Alco PAs, acquired from the Santa Fe in 1967, are left of a pair of EL EMD E8s, which supplemented the passenger power roster during winter months. The Colonie shops closed in 1987 when the D&H went into bankruptcy during the era of the Guilford administration and were finally razed in the summer of 2004. Nothing remains on the brownfield site today.

Plate 41   Delaware & Hudson Alco PAs #17, #18, and #19, Colonie shops, Watervliet, New York, April 13, 1988

Three of the four ex–Santa Fe Alco PA1s, acquired by D&H president Frederick C. "Buck" Dumaine in 1967 for use on the enhanced Montreal passenger services— the day *Laurentian* and the night *Montreal Sleeper*—pose in front of the extensive shop complex at Colonie, near Albany, New York. As the last survivors of a type of diesel passenger locomotive considered by many to be the best-looking model ever produced, they were widely photographed during their tenure on the D&H.

Plate 42   Erie Lackawanna freight train with E8 and GP7 on Starrucca Viaduct, Lanesboro, Pennsylvania, 1966

A displaced Erie Lackawanna E8 passenger diesel and a vintage road switcher labor upgrade across the historic Starrucca Viaduct near Lanesboro, Pennsylvania, on a late autumn afternoon. The 1,040-foot-long, 26-foot-wide,110-foot-high structure with seventeen stone arches was completed by the New York & Erie Railroad in 1848 using 800 men. Sturdily built, it has endured the vagaries of more than a century and a half of weather, as well as accommodating the much greater loads of modern trains and motive power.

Plate 43   Boston & Maine 4–6–2 #3713, Haverhill, Massachusetts, April 22, 1956

On its last run, Boston & Maine 4–6–2 #3713 streaks through a cut near Haverhill, Massachusetts, with a special train of rail enthusiasts bound for Portland, Maine, giving this elegant Pacific-type a fitting send-off into retirement. This locomotive has been preserved through the efforts of the late F. Nelson Blount and is being restored for future operation at Steamtown in Scranton, Pennsylvania, under the auspices of the National Park Service.

Plate 44   Canadian Pacific freight train and railroad crossing, eastern Quebec, February 23, 1957

Canadian winters are hard on men, machines, automobiles, and steam locomotives. Sandy Worthen's 1956 Oldsmobile waits at a road crossing in eastern Quebec for its occupants to return to its comfortable, warm interior after photographing a speeding westbound freight heading toward Sherbrooke from Megantic on the Saint John, New Brunswick–to–Montreal rail line. Shaughnessy traveled with Worthen extensively throughout Canada and the U.S. West. Worthen, according to rail photographer Greg McDonnell, "had a broad conceptual appreciation for history, as well as a refined understanding of a 'sense of place.'"

Plate 45   New York Central laborer cleans number board on an E8, Rensselaer, New York, January 17, 1961

A New York Central laborer cleans the number board on an EMD E8 passenger locomotive in the Rensselaer, New York, engine terminal. With the introduction of the diesel in the early 1950s the need for the huge roundhouse, for coaling and other servicing facilities that were located here, was eliminated. Diesels could run nonstop from Harmon, New York, to Chicago without refueling.

Plate 46   New York Central 4–6–0 #1199, St. Thomas, Ontario, August 18, 1956

One of the last operating steam locomotives on the vast New York Central system, 4–6–0 # 1199 moves onto the turntable at the St. Thomas, Ontario, roundhouse. This image was taken during an action-packed trip Shaughnessy made around Lake Erie with Phil Hastings and John Krause in the summer of 1956.

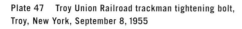

Plate 47   Troy Union Railroad trackman tightening bolt, Troy, New York, September 8, 1955

A trackman of the Troy Union Railroad (an NYC subsidiary) tightens a track joint bolt in the passenger station area as a Boston & Maine switcher crosses Broadway in Troy, New York. The Troy Union Railroad was established in 1854 to alleviate the growing traffic congestion associated with the four railroads serving the city at the time. It was half owned by the NYC, with the D&H and B&M sharing the remaining half in latter days. B&M SW1 #1115, an EMD product from 1946, is seen passing in the background after delivering a car to a spur served by the railroad on Adam Street, south of the station.

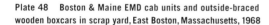

Plate 48   Boston & Maine EMD cab units and outside-braced wooden boxcars in scrap yard, East Boston, Massachusetts, 1968

The Boston & Maine's fleet of EMD passenger diesels and obsolete 1930s-vintage outside-braced wood-sided boxcars wait forlornly in an East Boston scrap yard. The B&M abandoned passenger service in 1968; all-steel boxcars replaced wooden ones as freight loads on the nation's railroads become heavier. Several boxcars pictured here ended service on shortline Wellsville, Addison & Galeton in the late 1970s.

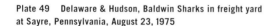

Plate 49   Delaware & Hudson, Baldwin Sharks in freight yard at Sayre, Pennsylvania, August 23, 1975

The pair of Baldwin-built Shark Nose diesels the Delaware & Hudson acquired during the administration of President C. B. Sterzing move through the Lehigh Valley's yard in Sayre, Pennsylvania, with #1205 in the lead, after bringing a connecting freight train west out of Binghamton, New York. The Baldwins were orphans on the D&H's roster and would not operate in multiple-unit control with other locomotives. These eccentricities were tolerated for special assignments and local use because the president liked them.

Plate 50   New York Central Alco RS3 #8350 on the West Side High Line, New York City, April 13, 1957

In this view we see New York Central Alco RS3 #8350 on the High Line that ran down the west side of Manhattan, serving produce warehouses and other businesses including a downtown facility of the U.S. Postal Service. The Empire State Building can be seen in the distance from this Eleventh Avenue & West 30th Street location. A portion of this route is being preserved and developed into a linear park by a group called the Friends of the Highline to augment the flourishing Chelsea art district nearby. The first section, from Gansevoort Street to 20th Street, is to open in 2008.

Plate 51   James A. Shaughnessy, posing as station agent, Mount Holly, Vermont, February 19, 1961

Jim's father, James A. Shaughnessy, poses as a veteran Rutland station agent, validating a ticket behind the screened window at Mount Holly, Vermont, amid the trappings of turn-of-the-century American transportation. Shaughnessy routinely posed family and friends in his images; he was one of the first American train photographers to stage photographs, replicating scenes from everyday railroading. In Jim's youth, he and his parents traveled New England together in pursuit of railroad subjects.

Plate 52   Delaware & Hudson freight train with EL SD45 #3606 approaches Mohawk River bridge, Schenectady, New York, 1975

A southbound Delaware & Hudson freight train from Mechanicville to Binghamton, New York, approaches the bridge over the Mohawk River in Schenectady behind run-through Erie Lackawanna locomotives. Many railroads had pooled power arrangements, where one railroad's locomotives would run over another's lines to eliminate the time it took to change engines at interchange points; this increased efficiency.

Plate 53   Central Vermont interior view of train shed, St. Albans, Vermont, 1956

This sweeping view of the interior of the great train shed, built in 1866–67, at Central Vermont's station in St. Albans, was an architectural rarity in the Northeast. Details of the curved roof trusses are interesting to take note of: the X-cross braces are in compression while iron rods comprise the horizontal members; 88-foot-long rods, called bowstrings, run between each end, with large nuts that can be loosened or tightened so the curve of the arch can be adjusted. While Shaughnessy appreciated the engineering aspects of such buildings, his archive shows that he rarely made these kinds of images. Interestingly enough, the photographer David Plowden also made photographs inside this imposing interior (see *The Iron Road*, Four Winds Press, 1978, p. 37).

Plate 54   Pennsylvania coal train powered by I-1-class 2–10–0 Decapod, Elmira Branch, Pennsylvania, May 5, 1957

A northbound Pennsylvania Railroad coal train powered by the hulk of an I-1-class 2–10–0 leaves a trail of soft coal smoke over the north-central Pennsylvania landscape as it heads toward Sodus Point, New York, on the Elmira Branch. This picturesque rural line, unlike the heavily industrialized areas usually associated with PRR routes, carried Appalachian bituminous coal to the gravity loading dock on the south shore of Lake Ontario. There, cars were pushed out on a pier extending into the lake and coal was dumped directly into the holds of waiting boats.

Plate 55   Nickel Plate engineer on 2–8–4 Berkshire #739 awaits "highball," Conneaut, Ohio, April 16, 1957

The engineer of an eastbound manifest freight train looks from the cab of his 2–8–4 Berkshire steam locomotive for the "highball" signal to start his run from Conneaut, Ohio, to Buffalo, New York.

Plate 56   Baltimore & Ohio local freight train gathering cars, Buckhannon, West Virginia, July 1, 1956

This view, taken from the passenger seat of Sandy Worthen's 1956 Oldsmobile, of a B&O local gathering loaded coal cars from area mines near Buckhannon, West Virginia, was an unusual type of railfan image when Jim made it in 1956. Train buffs, getting used to a new sense of mobility in the 1950s after the gas rationing of World War II, often utilized parts of cars—like a windshield— to frame their compositions.

Plate 57   Rutland freight train with RS3 #206 on high bridge across Walloomsac River, North Hoosick, New York, 1959

The freight train RC-2 bound from Rutland, Vermont, to Chatham, New York, is seen on the high bridge across the Walloomsac River in the village of North Hoosick illuminated by eight #50 flashbulbs, which generated 744,000 lumens. Shaughnessy had arranged with the railroad's dispatcher in Rutland to stop the train at a certain point on the bridge by signaling with a red flare to the engineer. Shaughnessy then instructed several of the seven helpers with him to open the lenses of three 4 x 5 Speed Graphics, alerting the remaining people to fire their handheld Graflex flash guns.

Plate 58   Central Vermont Alco RS3 #1859 on turntable, Saint Albans, Vermont, April 12, 1955

A Central Vermont Alco RS3 #1859 diesel road switcher rides on the St. Albans, Vermont, turntable outside the road's main operating and maintenance facility. During the early years of the steam-to-diesel transition, the two Alco RS3s on the CV were used principally on daily passenger trains but were later assigned to other Canadian National subsidiary lines when the CV received a fleet of new GM GP9s. This roundhouse and turntable are still in operation in 2008 and are now part of the New England Central Railroad.

Plate 59   Scrap yard scene of Southern Pacific RSD5s, Port of Albany, Albany, New York, December 1960

The Southern Pacific traded a fleet of its first-generation RSD5s diesel locomotives (pictured are #5284 and #5305) back to Alco (American Locomotive Company) in Schenectady, New York, for newer and more powerful models. The obsolete units worked their way east in revenue service on connecting railroads and were stripped of their reusable components at the Schenectady plant. The remaining parts—the old-model engine, hood, frame, and wiring—were transferred to a scrap dealer at the Port of Albany and were cut into pieces small enough to be fed into steel furnaces for recycling.

Plate 60   Boston & Maine E7 #3801 and passenger train, Troy, New York, 1958

"Hank," the veteran second trick Fulton Street crossing guard at the north end of the Troy Union Station, patiently waits for Boston & Maine train #62 to depart for Boston at 5 p.m. during the last month of B&M passenger service between Troy and Boston in 1958.

Plate 61   Delaware & Hudson brakeman signals on top of boxcar at Colonie yard, Watervliet, New York, 1961

A Delaware & Hudson brakeman (yardmaster Paul Mooney, posing for Shaughnessy) signals with his electric lantern for the power of the evening Whitehall fast freight to back down and couple onto its waiting train. This type of scene routinely occurred in American railroading until roof walks and full-ladders were banned by the FRA as safety hazards. The advent of two-way radios and better train brakes also made it unnecessary for brakemen to climb atop boxcars. Throughout his career, Shaughnessy applied the motifs of industrial photography to his work, such as the annual report imagery created by Chicago's Hedrich-Blessing firm during the same era.

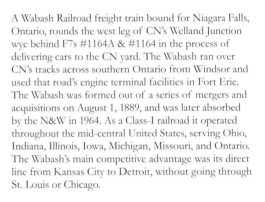

Plate 62   Wabash freight train with F7s #1164A and #1164, Welland Junction, Ontario, 1956

A Wabash Railroad freight train bound for Niagara Falls, Ontario, rounds the west leg of CN's Welland Junction wye behind F7s #1164A & #1164 in the process of delivering cars to the CN yard. The Wabash ran over CN's tracks across southern Ontario from Windsor and used that road's engine terminal facilities in Fort Erie. The Wabash was formed out of a series of mergers and acquisitions on August 1, 1889, and was later absorbed by the N&W in 1964. As a Class-I railroad it operated throughout the mid-central United States, serving Ohio, Indiana, Illinois, Iowa, Michigan, Missouri, and Ontario. The Wabash's main competitive advantage was its direct line from Kansas City to Detroit, without going through St. Louis or Chicago.

Plate 63   Canadian Pacific 4–6–2 #1217 outside roundhouse, Vallee Junction, Quebec, 1959

A Canadian Pacific 4–6–2 Pacific-type #1217 locomotive poses for night shots outside the Vallee Junction, Quebec, roundhouse between trips on the Quebec Central, a CP subsidiary.

Plate 64   Central New York Alco RS3 #101 and freight train near East Winfield, New York, December 31, 1988

A bleak and quiet winter's afternoon in central New York is broken by the sound of Alco RS3 #101 of the Central New York Railroad (a D&O subsidiary) as it brings a load of animal feed to a dealer in East Winfield, New York. The former Delaware, Lackawanna & Western's Richfield Springs Branch—22 miles in length—was acquired by the Delaware Otsego Corporation in 1973 and abandoned in 1995 due to insufficient traffic.

Plate 65   Union Pacific gas-turbine #57 and freight train near Cheyenne, Wyoming, August 20, 1957

A gas-turbine-powered Union Pacific freight roars west from Cheyenne, Wyoming, toward the continental divide at the summit of Sherman Hill. The UP was the only U.S. railroad to employ gas-turbine electric locomotives and ultimately had almost fifty, of various types and power output, in service. Built by General Electric, the first ten turbines arrived on the property in 1952.

Plate 66   New York, Ontario & Western freight train with EMD FT 1350hp diesels, led by #801, Kerryville, New York, 1956

A southbound New York, Ontario & Western train powered by a pair of early-model EMD FT 1350hp diesels crosses the divide between the east and west branch watersheds of the Delaware River at Kerryville near Apex, New York. Despite being one of the first American railroads to completely dieselize with the precedent-setting General Motors FT, the O&W did not save enough with this new railroad technology to offset the negative economic forces creeping into its territory. The railroad declared bankruptcy in early 1957, the first U.S. railroad of its size to do so.

Plate 67   Delaware & Hudson brakeman and Alco PAs, Colonie coach yard, Watervliet, New York, 1976

A brakeman guides a pair of Alco PA passenger locomotives toward the consist that will make up part of the *Laurentian* on a winter day, as fresh snow falls in the Colonie coach yard. These cars, including a diner, will be joined with connecting cars arriving in Albany from New York City for the daily trip to Montreal, Quebec. Delaware & Hudson's passenger service ended with the formation of Amtrak on May 1, 1971.

Plate 68   New York Central freight with Alco FA1 #1004, east of Chatham, New York, April 1958

A Boston-bound New York Central freight powered by Alco FA-1 #1004, running on the ex–Boston & Albany route, passes a unique road crossing sign (before the standard "X" configuration was adopted) three miles east of Chatham, New York. The NYC's northeastern rail network principally served the central New England area, while the competing railroads like the Boston & Maine and New Haven dealt with the northern and southern sections, respectively.

Plate 69   Baltimore & Ohio mechanic lubricates front valve gear mechanism on EM-1-class 2–8–8–4 articulated locomotive, Painesville, Ohio, 1955

A mechanic at the B&O's Painesville, Ohio, engine terminal uses an alamite gun to lubricate the front valve gear mechanism of an EM-1-class 2–8–8–4 articulated locomotive. The B&O's Lake Branch funneled bituminous coal north to Fairport Harbor on Lake Erie.

Plate 70   Tender of Grand Trunk Western locomotive, St. Albans, Vermont, April 12, 1955

In a rare kind of image for Shaughnessy—one that concentrates solely on the aesthetic qualities of steam engines—we see the side of a GTW locomotive tender in exquisite detail, beautifully rendered on 4 x 5 Royal Pan 400, Jim's preferred film choice. Railfan lensmen during the 1950s sensed intuitively that photographs could be multilayered and "read" in different ways. Pictures could be simple documents giving an accurate record of the object before the camera, be narrative in nature, or (as in this case) be aesthetically inclined, containing graphic details relying on notions of formalism.

Plate 71   Roundhouse laborer replenishing sand supply on Boston & Maine GP9 #1726, Mechanicville, New York, 1958

A third-trick roundhouse laborer replenishes the sand supply on a Boston & Maine GP9 at the sand house in the Mechanicville, New York, engine servicing facility. Mechanicville yard was built in the late 1880s and updated many times. It featured a "hump"-style classification yard with retarders in later years, and was completely abandoned in 1992. The D&H also had a freight yard in the area.

Plate 72   Bath & Hammondsport 44-ton center cab D-1 with freight train, Bath, New York, August 23, 1965

The Bath & Hammondsport Railroad was a short line running between its namesake communities in south-central New York state. Its principal item of traffic was wine (including sparkling wine) from the Taylor Winery in Hammondsport, hence the slogan on the cab of its 44T GE diesel: "The Champagne Route."

Plate 73   Norfolk & Western laborer lubricates driving rods of 4–8–2 locomotive, Hagerstown, Maryland, August 21, 1956

A terminal laborer lubricates the driving rods on a Norfolk & Western 4–8–2 in Hagerstown, Maryland, the northern terminus of that road's Shenandoah Valley line. Shaughnessy often saw the railroad landscape as social space. As his work progressed he became very interested in the interrelationships between man and machine and the photographic possibilities they presented.

Plate 74   New York Central 4–6–0 #1290, St. Thomas, Ontario, August 18, 1956

A rare steam locomotive of the New York Central's Canada Southern subsidiary, used on the weight-restricted St. Clair subdivision, sits by the water plugs at the St. Thomas, Ontario, engine house between runs. This turn-of-the-century locomotive, and a sister, operated long after their famous and more modern Hudson and Niagara brethren were retired and scrapped. 4–6–0 #1290 was built in 1900 and scrapped in May 1957. This image was one of many made by Shaughnessy while he, Phil Hastings, and John Krause traveled together shooting the last of steam around Lake Erie. In a three-day period they encountered NYC 4–6–0s, rusting hulks of DT&I 2–8–4s, ex–B&M 4–8–2s, and Nickel Plate Berkshires.

Plate 75   New York Central freight train with Alco FA1 #1034 entering State Line tunnel, Canaan, New York, June 9, 1957

An eastbound freight on the New York Central's Boston line or B&A—the Boston & Albany—merged into the NYC system in 1900—enters one of the twin State Line tunnels near Canaan, New York, west of the New York/Massachusetts state line. This is the principal route from Selkirk yard near Albany, New York, to central Massachusetts. A large amount of freight traffic to Boston funnels into the southern portion of New England over these tracks since the closure of New Haven's freight line to Maybrook, New York, in May 1974. That year the Hudson River bridge at Poughkeepsie burned, sealing off a direct rail line into central New England.

Plate 76   Boston & Maine, Little Hoosac Tunnel, North Adams, Massachusetts, 1956

Boston & Maine's Little Hoosac Tunnel just south of downtown North Adams, Massachusetts, is located two miles from its better-known 25,081-foot counterpart stretched beneath the spine of the Berkshire range. Shaughnessy took occasional photographs, without trains, that explored the railroad landscape. This image was made intentionally for an article on tunnels he did with Richard Sanders Allen that appeared in the June 1960 issue of *Trains*.

Plate 77   Canadian National engine crew on 2–8–2 #3496, Fort Erie, Ontario, September 22, 1956

The engine crew of a Canadian National freight about to depart Fort Erie, Ontario (with 2–8–2 #3496 on the head end), awaits the signal from their conductor that they may proceed. Fort Erie was one of the major entry points into Canada for rail traffic from the United States. There was also considerable rail traffic generated by local industry, due to the plentiful power provided by nearby Niagara Falls. Shaughnessy made several iconic images at night; this is a classic.

Plate 78   Central Vermont station agent handing up orders, East Northfield, Massachusetts, April 12, 1954

The station agent at East Northfield, Massachusetts, is seen here handing up orders to the southbound local freight coming through the station. Before two-way radios and remote-control signals, train orders were telegraphed, or later telephoned, to operator/agents in stations along the route. Three copies would be handwritten, attached to a loop of string, and strung onto a Y-shaped holder. The passing train would not stop and the orders for further movements down the line would be handed to a member of the locomotive crew "on the fly" into an outstretched arm; the conductor would also get a set in the same fashion as the caboose swung by. Today, two-way radio communication has replaced the agents and the "flimsies" (as the translucent paper orders were called).

Plate 79   Erie Lackawanna and Delaware & Hudson freight trains, Starrucca Viaduct, Lanesboro, Pennsylvania, 1972

The historic Starrucca Viaduct in Lanesboro, Pennsylvania, sees the passing of an eastbound EL train (symbol NE-74) heading to New Jersey, while a southbound D&H train (symbol RW-6) passes underneath on its way to connections at Wilkes-Barre, Pennsylvania. The Erie Railroad built the Starrucca Viaduct—1,040 feet long, with seventeen great stone arches rising 110 feet above the ground—in 1848. Modern freight trains still cross this noble structure, an engineering marvel from the nineteenth century.

Plate 80   Boston & Maine laborer washing windows of passenger E7 #3814, Bangor, Maine, April 10, 1955

A Boston & Maine EMD E7 2000hp passenger unit #3814 has its windshield cleaned in Bangor, Maine, while serving the joint B&M–Maine Central pool passenger service between central Maine and Boston.

Plate 81   Norfolk & Western Y6b 2–8–8–2 #2129 and helper crew, Boaz siding, near Vinton, Virginia, August 8, 1957

An N&W helper engine crewman waits by the telephone shanty at Boaz siding near Vinton, Virginia, at the western side of the heavy Blue Ridge Mountains grade, to push heavy coal trains over the hill on their journey to tidewater ports. They kept in contact with the train dispatcher over the telephone to be ready for approaching coal trains.

Plate 82   Canadian Pacific Jubilee type 4–4–4, #2927, Sutton, Quebec, December 26, 1955

On a below-zero night in Sutton, Quebec, just north of the U.S. border above Vermont, a Canadian Pacific Jubilee type 4–4–4, #2927, awaits the call to take the early morning passenger train into Montreal.

Plate 83   Canadian Pacific 4–6–2 #2236 and engineer Frank Bunker, west of Galt, Ontario, August 1957

Engineer Frank Bunker leans out of the cab window of Canadian Pacific 4–6–2 #2236 as he rolls up the hill west of Galt, Ontario, toward the summit at Orr's Lake. This 4–6–2, plus the Royal Hudson behind, has fourteen heavy passenger cars to deliver to Windsor for an expected surge in holiday traffic.

Plate 84   Baltimore & Ohio EM-1-class 2–8–8–4, near Painesville, Ohio, 1955

The Baltimore & Ohio Railroad had a number of large, powerful steam locomotives employed to handle heavy coal trains on Appalachian grades. The elongated boiler of a Yellowstone-type class EM-1 2–8–8–4 stretches ahead, seen from the coal pile in the tender, as it waits to assist a Lake Erie–bound coal train over the rolling elevations of northern Ohio. Shaughnessy liked to occasionally make unconventional views of steam locomotives, an approach that helped redefine rail photography in the 1950s.

Plate 85   Canadian National Spadina Avenue engine-servicing facility, Toronto, Ontario, March 10, 1957

A low winter sun illuminates Canadian National steam locomotives at the company's Spadina Avenue engine-servicing facility in downtown Toronto, as they wait to be dispatched on afternoon passenger runs out of the city. After complete dieselization of the CN, this service area was closed and is now the site of the spectacular CN Tower, one of the tallest freestanding structures in the world.

Plate 86   Central Vermont 0–8–0 #501 on turntable, Brattleboro, Vermont, April 21, 1956

On one of the first trips Shaughnessy made with Phil Hastings, the two stopped in Brattleboro, Vermont, at the CV roundhouse on the eve of a B&M #3713 excursion run. With time to kill, the two photographers, aided by a friendly hostler who spotted CV 0–8–0 switcher #501 on the turntable, made open flash and time exposures well past midnight. The yard switcher was a fixture on the local railroad scene, servicing the area's industries as well as making up the local to Palmer that departed each morning.

Plate 87   Norfolk & Western 2–8–8–2 and merchandise freight, east of Roanoke, Virginia, August 6, 1957

An eastbound Norfolk & Western merchandise train is helped over the summit of the Blue Ridge Mountains east of Roanoke, Virginia, by one of the road's fleet of powerful mallet-type 2–8–8–2s, which were built in N&W's own shops in Roanoke after World War II. This railroad carried millions of tons of coal every year from West Virginia mines to the coal docks on the Atlantic Ocean at Lambert's Point, near Norfolk, Virginia.

Plate 88   Pennsylvania station agent Louise Overhiser handing up orders to 2–10–0 #4512, Watkins Glen, New York, August 20, 1960

Louise Overhiser, the block operator at the Pennsylvania's Watkins Glen, New York, station hands orders up to the engineer of a big 386,000-pound I-1-class 2–10–0 #4512 as it thunders past her with a string of empty hopper cars. This train is returning to Appalachian coal country from the loading docks at Sodus Point on Lake Ontario east of Rochester, New York. The crew of an Elmira Branch local freight wait for the passing train to clear so they can come out of a side track and continue northward. Overhiser was a tenured employee from World War II days, during an era when many women filled jobs not normally associated with their gender. In their own way these women were as brave and determined as the husbands and brothers that went off to defend their country in wartime.

Plate 89   Central Vermont station and train shed, St Albans, Vermont, March 28, 1956

The Central Vermont station and covered train shed at St. Albans, Vermont, looms large over the sizable mass of Canadian National 4–8–4 #6173 protruding from the first portal of the structure. The overnight all-sleeper consist between Montreal, Quebec, and Washington, DC, shown in the timetable as train #20 the *Washingtonian*, had a fabled history. Though it had begun running even prior to the Eighteenth Amendment's prohibition on liquor, it was known in many circles affectionately as the *Bootlegger* for the illegal contraband that often found its way on board, en route to the speakeasies of New York City. The CN Northern steam locomotive will haul the sleeping, or perhaps slightly inebriated, passengers over the Green Mountains (which are part of the Appalachian chain) to White River Junction, Vermont, where the train will be turned over to the B&M, New Haven, and Pennsylvania railroads for the remainder of the trek to the capital.

Plate 90   Pennsylvania freight train with F7s, unknown location on Elmira Branch, Pennsylvania, August 20, 1965

The Pennsylvania Railroad's Elmira Branch, once the scene of spectacular steam locomotive operations, turned more tranquil when its operation transitioned to diesels in the early 1960s. Here EMD F7 freight units pass a barn in northern Pennsylvania displaying a faded ad for Red Man chewing tobacco, an emblem from a bygone era when advertising had an innocent, less politically correct tone. The Penn Central petitioned to abandon its Elmira Branch after the devastating effects of Hurricane Agnes in 1972.

Plate 91   Norfolk & Western coal train, east of Roanoke, Virginia, 1957

An eastbound Norfolk & Western 150-car coal train fights gravity to the summit of the Blue Ridge Mountains east of Roanoke, Virginia, with the aid of three huge articulated locomotives—two leading and one pushing. Note the accumulation of sand along the uphill track, placed on the rail ahead of the driving wheels by the lead 2–8–8–2 Y6b engine to increase traction.

Plate 92   Nickel Plate train order operator prepares to hand up "flimsies," Brocton, New York, 1957

A train order operator at Brocton, New York, prepares to hand orders to an approaching train bound for Chicago from Buffalo on the Nickel Plate's famous lakeshore route.

Plate 93   New York Central freight with Alco FA #1085, Pattersonville, New York, December 10, 1955

The unique architecture of the old West Shore railroad, which became part of the New York Central system, is reflected in the station building at Pattersonville, New York, as an Alco-powered freight rolls east toward the Selkirk classification yards.

Plate 94   St. Johnsbury & Lamoille County outside-braced wood boxcar and covered bridge, Swanton, Vermont, October 15, 1955

An outside-braced wood boxcar of the St. Johnsbury & Lamoille County railroad sits on a siding in the small yard at Swanton, Vermont, awaiting the move to a customer in Morrisville, Vermont. A covered bridge, a familiar architectural feature of the New England countryside, stands in the distance. This tableau accurately captures the essence of a short line in decline—as well as suggesting a sense of place, and the defining textures of the Northeast railroad landscape Shaughnessy knew well. Railfan photographers in the 1950s began to explore the total rail environment, becoming more sensitive to elements beyond the engines and hardware. Shaughnessy was one of the photographers at the forefront of this movement, which broadens our understanding and awareness of railroading visual culture.

Plate 95   Canadian National switchman and 4–6–0 #1586, Palmerston, Ontario, February 15, 1958

Under blustery skies, a switchman waits while venerable CN 4–6–0 #1586 (which is better than twice his age, having been built in 1913 for the Canadian Northern) makes up its train to service one of several branch lines radiating out of Palmerston, Ontario. The spring of 1959 would be the final swan song for CN steam in the Palmerston area. Seven ten-wheelers alone were active in the yard there and found themselves on mixed trains and way freights going to Southampton, Owen Sound, and Kincardine. Shaughnessy had a special penchant for Canadian railroading and perhaps did his strongest work there. Phil Hastings and Craig Wentworth often accompanied him to photograph the southern Ontario railroad scene during steam's final hour. Palmerston was a favorite location.

Plate 96   Pennsylvania Railroad and laborer washing GG1, Washington, DC, June 18, 1960

A laborer washes one of the famous Raymond Lowey–styled GG1 electric locomotives between runs to New York City. The Ivy City engine terminal in Washington, DC, was the south end of the PRR's electric operations. 139 GG1s were built between 1934 and 1944, many of them at the PRR shops in Altoona, Pennsylvania. These locomotives generated 4620 continuous horsepower and ran upwards of 100 mph. GG1 #4879 made the last regularly scheduled revenue run on Friday, October 28, 1983.

Plate 97   Illinois Central hostler approaches 2–8–2 #2137, Paducah, Kentucky, September 1, 1957

An Illinois Central hostler approaches 2–8–2 #2137 in the Paducah, Kentucky, engine terminal to move it into the servicing area, where the firebox will be cleaned and a supply of coal and water loaded; mechanical parts will also be lubricated, with the entire locomotive readied for the next day's work. In the 1950s, some railfans were able to sign waivers that absolved the railroad company from legal responsibility while they were on the property. Paducah, home to Illinois Central's major repair shop and engine-servicing facility, was one such location.

Plate 98   Denver & Rio Grande FT #5414 and water column, Alamosa, Colorado, October 2, 1959

Denver & Rio Grande FT #5414 freight locomotive spends the night resting near the water column in Alamosa, Colorado—a mechanical and industrial relic from the steam era used to slake the thirst of 2–8–2 Mikados. The yard in Alamosa was the scene of dual-gauge track—narrow and standard—which made this unusual juxtaposition possible. Lucius Beebe was enmored with Shaughnessy's night work and used it repeatedly in his own books. This image originally appeared in his *Rio Grande to the Rockies*.

Plate 99   Pennsylvania freight train and operator handing up orders, Leolyn, Pennsylvania, May 5, 1957

The train order operator at Leolyn, Pennsylvania, hands a copy of orders to the fireman on a 2–10–0 leading a northbound PRR coal train on the Elmira Branch during an early spring snow squall.

Plate 100   Delaware & Hudson *Laurentian* with Alco PA and man with umbrella, Port Henry, New York, May 10, 1970

A passenger, definitely not carrying designer luggage, waits on a rainy day to board the approaching southbound Delaware & Hudson's *Laurentian* at Port Henry, New York, situated on the west shore of Lake Champlain. This train, and an overnight sleeper service, ran daily between New York City and Montreal with connections through Albany. The town is still serviced daily by Amtrak's *Adirondack*. The PAs were the favorites of D&H president Sterzing and area railfans. The D&H ultimately had four ex–Santa-Fe engines that were refurbished, repainted, and put on the roster. Port Henry was once a busy industrial area with a large blast furnace that processed an iron ore called magnetite, found within deep Adirondack mines.

Plate 101   Rutland freight train RC-2 with RS3 #208 on bridge over Walloomsac River, near state line, New York, 1959

The overnight Rutland Railway freight train RC-2 from Rutland, Vermont, to Chatham, New York, is seen on the bridge crossing the Walloomsac River near the New York state line, on the B&M's Bennington Branch. This train once traveled its own rails through the eastern edge of Rensselaer County in New York to reach Chatham and carried milk destined for New York City markets. When this line—affectionately called the Cork Screw due to a curvy section near Bennington—was abandoned in 1953, an alternate route via the B&M and NYC was established.

Plate 102   Pennsylvania freight train with 2–10–0 #4587 and operator handing up orders, Elmira, New York, 1957

A southbound freight powered by 2–10–0 #4587, one of the PRR's most numerous and utilitarian steam locomotive types (there were 565 I-1-class 2–10–0s listed on PRR's roster), will receive orders from the Kendall tower operator at the southern end of the Southport yard in Elmira, New York. While this was a rare type of image for Shaughnessy, he did do occasional synchronized "light-up-the-night" photography for a handful of pictures. He even once contemplated constructing an elaborate battery-capacitor flash unit like O. Winston Link used to stop action, but soon jettisoned the idea for an approach pared for thrift and simplicity: available light, time exposure, and "painted" open flash.

Plate 103   Canadian National 4–8–4 getting its tender filled, Turcot engine terminal, Montreal, Quebec, 1954

A roundhouse worker at Canadian National's Turcot engine terminal in Montreal fills the tender of a CN 4–8–4 amid the swirling steam and smoke of other waiting locomotives on this –12°F winter's day. Turcot yard, with its huge locomotive servicing facility, was the principal railroad center for CN freight operations in Montreal, and served the visiting locomotives of the Rutland and Central Vermont railroads.

Plate 104   Reading 4–8–4 with freight train exiting off of Rockville Bridge, Harrisburg, Pennsylvania, 1956

A Reading Railroad T-1-class 4–8–4 curves its train off the Rockville Bridge that crosses the Susquehanna River west of Harrisburg and approaches the Pennsylvania Railroad's Enola yard. Ironically, the PRR (which owned more steam locomotives than any other American railroad) embarked on its dieselization plan abruptly. It retired too many steam engines prematurely and got caught short-handed when traffic surged, requiring it to lease steam locomotives from a neighboring competitor, Reading.

Plate 105   Grand Trunk 2–8–2 #3709 and freight train, Sherbrooke, Quebec, February 1957

A Grand Trunk freight runs along the St. Francis River in Sherbrooke, Quebec, on the century-and-a-half old route of the Grand Trunk Railway, opened in 1852, to connect the Atlantic Ocean at Portland, Maine, with the Great Lakes basin at Montreal, Quebec.

Plate 106   Canadian Pacific 2–8–0 #3488 switch engine, St. Luc yard, Montreal, Quebec, October 11, 1956

A veteran Canadian Pacific switch engine moves a van (caboose) at Montreal's St. Luc yard in an impressive display of smoke and steam. Shaughnessy loved the action around yards and engine facilities, with the ever-shifting possibilities they offered for dramatic photography. This image, made with a 2¼ Rollei, shows Shaughnessy in a fluid photographic moment.

Plate 107   Baltimore & Ohio coal train crosses Nickel Plate mainline, Painesville, Ohio, September 25, 1955

A B&O coal train crosses the NKP mainline en route to Fairport, Ohio, where the coal out of West Virginia will be transferred to lake boats for movement to customers in the Great Lakes Basin. Here in a perfectly timed exposure a B&O caboose, and its conductor framed in the gantry way, rolls over the diamond at Painesville, Ohio. Shaughnessy occasionally employed low-camera angles— "a worm's-eye view"—to dramatic effect, lending a "you-are-there" feel to the photograph.

Plate 108   Union Pacific freight train with "Big Boy" #4009 crosses east side of continental divide, Dale Junction, Wyoming, August 20, 1957

The Union Pacific Railroad operated twenty-five of the largest steam locomotives ever built, 4–8–8–4s appropriately called "Big Boy." Here one of their number hauls a long freight train up the east side of the continental divide near Dale Junction on Sherman Hill, between Cheyenne and Laramie, Wyoming. It is running on the new lower-elevation line built after World War II— a line mostly used by heavy westbound traffic.

Plate 109   Canadian Pacific double-headed 2–8–2s on freight train, Cookshire, Quebec, February 11, 1956

Double-headed 2–8–2s on the point of a Canadian Pacific freight train at Cookshire, Quebec, give off a spectacular display of power as they get their train rolling again after a brief water stop. A local farmer, employing his horse-drawn wagon, moves coal from a parked hopper car to a local bin, to help ward off the effects of the cold Canadian winter. This photograph, perhaps the photographer's favorite, which he calls *Four Horses—Two Iron*, was one of many images he made featuring animals.

Plate 110   Canadian National local passenger train #175 with 4–6–0 #1564 prepares to depart Palmerston, Ontario, 1958

A local CN passenger train prepares to depart Palmerston, Ontario, for Owen Sound. Less-than-carload freight is being loaded into the train's baggage car. This image comes from one of the eight trips Shaughnessy took with Phil Hastings in the mid-1950s. (For a similar image by Hastings taken at the same time, see *Starlight on the Rails*, p. 51.) The two photographers met in 1954 at an impromtu gathering at Hastings's house near Selkirk, New York. They undoubtedly influence each other's photographic style and maintained a friendship until Phil's untimely death in 1987.

Plate 111   Canadian National 4–8–4 #6258 on ready track with waiting crew members, Brockville, Ontario, 1958

Two crew members wait to board 4–8–4 #6258 on the ready track in the engine terminal area at Brockville, Ontario. Shaughnessy routinely asked railroaders to pose in his images; he was interested in trying to replicate scenes he had previously seen, always striving for naturalism. Here two railroaders stand still while the photographer makes a thirty-second time exposure with his 4 x 5 Speed Graphic.

Plate 112   New Haven *Patriot* powered by Alco PAs crosses Canton Viaduct, Canton, Massachusetts, April 19, 1958

A southbound New Haven passenger train, the *Patriot*—powered by a pair of the beloved Alco PAs—crosses the solid granite edifice of the Canton Viaduct in Canton, Massachusetts, several miles south of Boston. This train was one of many offered by NH on its southern New England route between Boston and New York City.

Plate 113   New York Central passenger train, Castleton, New York, April 1956

A northbound New York Central passenger train passes under the NYC's Castleton Bridge—also known as the Alfred E. Smith Memorial Bridge or Castleton cutoff. It was built in 1924 to connect with a large classification yard in Selkirk, New York, that would act as a bypass to alleviate traffic congestion in West Albany yard caused by capacity problems and a steep grade to the west that required helper service. This was one of forty daily passenger trains on the Water Level Route. On this particular day, the private car of noted railroad book author Lucius Beebe was on the rear end.

Plate 114   Canadian National passenger train behind 4–8–4 #6223, Welland Junction, Ontario, August 4, 1957

A special train from Toronto carrying patrons to the race-track in Fort Erie, Ontario, rounds the east leg of the wye at Welland Junction behind Northern #6223, one of the great fleet of CN 4–8–4s, which numbered over 200.

Plate 115   Canadian Pacific 2–8–2 #5396 and freight train in snowstorm, Lennoxville, Quebec, January 29, 1954

A Canadian Pacific 2–8–2 leads an eastbound freight past the Lennoxville, Quebec, station platform as it makes its way toward Saint John, New Brunswick, on the line that carried vast quantities of export grain during the months the St. Lawrence River was choked with ice.

Plate 116   Denver & Rio Grande freight with 2–8–2 #487, Romeo, Colorado, 1959

The Denver & Rio Grande Western's dual gauge—three-foot and standard placed together, using three rails rather than the usual two—paralleled the straight highway between Alamosa and Antonito and provided a unique opportunity to drive along with a moving train for almost 28 miles. Here a narrow-gauge 2–8–2 rolls south with a trainload of pipe bound for oil fields near Farmington, New Mexico.

Plate 117   St. Johnsbury & Lamoille County mixed train #44, Lamoille Valley, Vermont, September 1955

In one of the photographer's favorite images, the St. Johnsbury & Lamoille County's daily mixed train #44 rolls east through the Lamoille Valley of northern Vermont on its 96-mile journey to St. Johnsbury, while horses—two choosing to race the train—enjoy one of the lush pastures in the area. The tranquility of their domain will not be disturbed until the same time tomorrow by this lightly traveled shortline railroad.

Plate 118   St. Johnsbury & Lake Champlain freight piloted by 70-ton GE diesels #46 and #48, Wolcott, Vermont, 1967

The St. Johnsbury & Lake Champlain Railroad—later called the St. Johnsbury & Lamoille County—was the middle link in a railroad system built in the late 1870s called the Portland & Ogdensburg. This stretched from the Atlantic to the Great Lakes over a route involving difficult and hilly terrain, including a steep climb through Crawford Notch in the White Mountains of New Hampshire. Unfortunately, the line never achieved the success its founders had hoped for. In this image three light 70-ton GE diesels haul a westbound train through one of five wooden covered bridges the railroad encountered in Vermont. These unique artifacts of New England architecture remained in use almost to the end of operations, which ceased in the early 1990s. Shaughnessy routinely photographed shortlines in the area.

Plate 119   Central Vermont train shed demolition, St. Albans, Vermont, September 29, 1963

This image shows the tearing down of the landmark CV train shed at St. Albans, Vermont. With the demise of passenger service, the great covered area was no longer needed. The structure had served faithfully since 1867 but, unfortunately, was in need of expensive repairs. The 88-foot trusses, invented and designed by William Howe in 1840, were used primarily on bridges; their use here as curved interior roof supports was unusual. Built on the ground and raised into place by rigging, the trusses were curved on the top and bottom to follow the roof contour. Shaughnessy made occasional documentary pictures of architecture and locomotives being demolished or scrapped. Some of these images, especially the ones made at St. Albans during the razing of the train shed (there are fifteen images in total), are reminiscent of Civil War photographs made by George Barnard documenting the destruction caused by General William Tecumseh Sherman's "march to the sea" in 1864.

Plate 120   Canadian National 4–8–4 #6173 emerging from the train shed at St. Albans, Vermont, November 1956

Canadian National 4–8–4 #6173 pokes its nose out of the covered train shed of the Central Vermont's St. Albans station after bringing the day train, the *Ambassador,* from Montreal, Quebec. This unique architectural feature of the CV was constructed to keep passengers out of inclement Northeast weather. It stood until 1963; costly upkeep and general deterioration took their toll. The station and shed were built out of local brick by contractors Harris & Hawkins of Springfield, Massachusetts, in 1866–67.

Plate 121   Baltimore & Ohio 2–8–8–4 #7611 and freight train, Failes Spur, Ohio, 1955

The ground trembles as two 932,700-pound Baltimore & Ohio articulated 2–8–8–4 EM-1-class Yellowstone-type locomotives pound past a whitewashed fence in northern Ohio as they start a 6,400-ton coal train out of the helper siding, at Failes Spur, 30 miles south of Painesville, Ohio, on the Lake Branch. Their thirty-two driving wheels produce 230,000 pounds of tractive effort to move the train over the hilly countryside toward the south shore of Lake Erie.

Plate 122   Canadian National RSC13 road switcher #1703 and 2–8–0 #2631, Stratford, Ontario, 1959

The roundhouse turntable at Stratford, Ontario, finds MLW 1000hp model RSC13 road switcher #1703 almost obscured by the smoke and steam of veteran 2–8–0 Consolidation #2631, which had been assigned to this terminal since August 1958 and would end its career here after the onset of dieselization. The terminal hostler is returning from stoking the fire on the 2–8–0 in preparation for another day's work in the area.

Plate 123   Boston & Maine 4–6–2 #3705 with southbound *Green Mountain Flyer*, North Bennington, Vermont, 1952

Boston & Maine 4–6–2 Pacific #3705 blasts out of the station at North Bennington, Vermont, with the southbound *Green Mountain Flyer* down from Montreal, Quebec. This train had traversed the west side of Vermont, will make connections at Troy, New York, and then resume its journey to New York City over the NYC on the Water Level Route along the Hudson River. Although this was a Rutland train, it was periodically powered by B&M locomotives and crews to balance the shared costs associated with trackage rights agreements.

Plate 124   Rutland brakeman and freight train, with RS3 #202 waiting on siding, Vergennes, Vermont, September 1955

A Rutland brakeman patiently waits by a turnout he's just aligned for the passing track at Vergennes, Vermont, so the Burlington-bound counterpart to his Alburgh local, waiting in the distance, can pass on this single-track railroad. The Rutland was a rural common carrier running the length of western Vermont and across the top of northern New York to Ogdensburg, through pastoral landscapes. Milk was the major commodity the Rutland hauled, as the principal industry in the region was dairy farming. Most of this traffic evaporated with the introduction of refrigerated trucks on state highways in the 1940s.

Plate 125   Canadian Pacific 4–6–2 #1257 and local passenger train #40, Sherbrooke, Quebec, February 1957

In a moody night image, Canadian Pacific's all-stops train, local #40, from Montreal to Megantic, Quebec, pauses at the Sherbrooke station while G5c-class Pacific #1257 simmers on the head end and sends warming steam to the cars behind. Passengers mill around on the station platform, creating an evocative scene with almost Hitchcockian overtones. Shaughnessy found Sherbrooke a well-situated place for his railfanning activities; it was a favorite haunt.

Plate 126   Canadian National FPA4 #6786 and grain elevator, Chamy, Quebec, August 27, 1964

In a prairie-like setting, CN's Montreal-to-Quebec City Champlain (which used Reading *Crusader* stainless steel cars) rolls past a grain elevator—a familiar piece of architecture in the wheat-producing areas of the U.S. and Canada. This view, taken at Chamy, Quebec, is where the train will diverge from the mainline to the Maritimes, crossing the St. Lawrence River on the famous Pont de Quebec (Quebec Bridge) into the capital city of La Belle Province.

Plate 127   Union Pacific freight train piloted by 4–8–4 #800, eastern Nebraska, July 26, 1955

One of Union Pacific's fleet of forty-five big 4–8–4 Northern-type dual service locomotives, #800 leads an eastbound freight through the cornfields of eastern Nebraska heading for North Platte and Omaha. This rail line paralleled U.S. Highway 30 for many miles. The high volume of traffic running on this transcontinental route, once part of the original alignment of the Oregon Trail, provided a never-ending parade of trains to amuse drivers.

Plate 128   St. Johnsbury & Lamoille County GE 70-ton diesels #55 and #46 with freight train, Morrisville, Vermont, August 21, 1967

The fog is lifting on the Lamoille River at Morrisville, Vermont, as three St. Johnsbury & Lamoille County GE 70-ton diesels bring the daily mixed train—running between the CV connection at Swanton and the MEC at St. Johnsbury—into town. The 96-mile short line was once the middle section of an ambitious scheme to connect Portland, Maine, with the Great Lakes at Ogdensburg, New York, in the late 1870s (for most of the twentieth century, the Maine Central and Rutland were the eastern and western sections, respectively). The Portland and Ogdensburg Railroad, as a conceptual entity, gradually disappeared, with the demise of the Rutland in 1961 and the Lamoille Valley (successor to the St. J & LC) in the early 1990s, this after several failed attempts by the state of Vermont to financially sustain the line.

Plate 129   New York Central freight and six Alcos led by FA #1042, Voorheesville, New York, April 1962

A New York Central freight, powered by six Alcos led by FA #1042, approaches the D&H's Binghamton line diamond at Voorheesville, New York, a crossing guarded by a station built in 1889. The station's architectural style—a modernized Romanesque—was of a unique variety built by the original New York, West Shore & Buffalo Railway.

Plate 130   Boston & Maine freight MB-6 at the east end of yard complex, Mechanicville, New York, January 1960

A switchman hastens to make up a Boston-bound freight, symbol MB-6, at the throat of the vast Boston & Maine yard complex in Mechanicville, New York. Geep #1710 manages the switching moves on an icicle-filled night. Shaughnessy, accustomed to cold by a lifetime in the Northeast, routinely made night images in subzero weather.

Plate 131   Chicago, Burlington & Quincy 4–8–4 #5634 starts train in interchange yard at Zearing, Illinois, 1956

A Chicago, Burlington & Quincy O-5-class 4–8–4 starts its train moving out of Zearing, Illinois, after interchanging cars with the NYC at the westernmost point of its far-flung system. Several O-5 4–8–4s, 4–6–4s, and 2–10–4s were pulled out of temporary storage to help move a bumper grain crop in the fall of 1956. Steam excursion fantrips with sister 0-5 #5632 ran on the CB&Q between 1958 and 1964.

Plate 132   Delaware & Hudson freight train WR-1 with caboose, Ballston Spa, New York, 1959

Northbound Delaware & Hudson's train WR-1 and its caboose roll across the big fill near Ballston Spa, New York, on a stretch of track constructed in the early 1950s to eliminate nine grade crossings in the township. This freight train, rolling below a sky dotted with cumulous clouds, carried mainly empty paper product and newsprint cars back to Canadian mills for reloading. The WR symbol stands for the starting and ending points of the trip on the D&H-Wilkes–Barre, Pennsylvania, and Rouses Point, New York.

Plate 133   New York, Ontario & Western station agent, Campbell Hall, New York, 1956

A station agent in the NYO&W's Campbell Hall, New York, station is surrounded by a classic tableau from the halcyon days of the industry—standard clock, telegraph key, and train sheets. Little did the agent know he had less than a year left on the payroll. Operations ceased on the NYO&W in March 1957.

Plate 134   Rutland depot interior and operator's desk, Vergennes, Vermont, 1961

Looking through the agent's bay window at the Rutland's Vergennes, Vermont, station, closed due to a labor dispute, one finds the trappings of his profession—a telephone, dirty windows, train sheet, and other paperwork—just where he left them when the railroad went on strike on September 25, 1961. The Rutland was eventually abandoned because of an impasse between labor and management.

Plate 135   Delaware & Hudson 4–6–6–4 on freight train (symbol AB-4) in Watervliet, New York, 1950

A cold, clear winter's day finds a Delaware & Hudson 4–6–6–4 "Challenger"-type on freight train (symbol AB-4) in Watervliet, New York, heading from Albany to Binghamton via Mechanicville. The steam coming from its melodious whistle is obscuring part of the smoke stack as the engineer blows for the crossing as the train approaches Elm Street. Many of Shaughnessy's early negatives from 1946–50 indicate an openness to a different vision, like that shown here. One of Shaughnessy's more evocative images, it hints at "atmospheric" effect—a trait that soon shifts instead toward a clear delineation and accurate rendering of what lay before the camera. This image was made with a Busch Pressman 2¼ x 3¼ camera, which used cut sheet film.

Plate 136   Denver & Rio Grande Mikado 2–8–2 #483, Chama, New Mexico, September 28, 1958

A three-foot-gauge 2–8–2 simmers overnight just outside the engine house in Chama, New Mexico, and will be ready to tackle the stiff grades on Rio Grande's Cumbres Pass line in the morning. This narrow-gauge three-foot line over 10,015-foot Cumbres Pass was built in 1880 as the San Juan Extension of the D&RGW and went 199.8 miles from Alamosa to Durango, crossing the Colorado–New Mexico boundary ten times in the process. In 1970 a 64-mile section between Chama, New Mexico, and Antonito, Colorado, was jointly purchased by both states and leased to a tourist operator called the Cumbres & Toltec Scenic Railroad. These trains now operate during the summer and autumn months, affording passengers and railfans a view of the most scenic aspects of the Rio Grande narrow-gauge empire.

Plate 137   Canadian National 2–8–0 #2381 and Wabash EMD F7A #1160 at engine terminal, Fort Erie, Ontario, 1955

On a crisp winter morning, wispy plumes of steam shroud the smokebox of Canadian National 2–8–0 Consolidation #2381 as it sits in the Fort Erie, Ontario, engine terminal alongside a Wabash Railroad EMD F7A. These engines-in-wait suggest the steam-to-diesel transition coming to North American railroading. The Wabash train has just arrived from Windsor, Ontario.

Plate 138   Delaware & Hudson engineer boards GE-built U23B #2318, Mechanicville, New York, March 8, 1975

A Delaware & Hudson engineer boards his GE-built U23B #2318 locomotive on a threatening winter day at the Mechanicville, New York, roundhouse for a trip to Binghamton. After the decline of anthracite coal for domestic heating, the bulk of traffic on the D&H was the movement of various types of merchandise, including paper products, between New England and the Midwest. The D&H's connection with the B&M at Mechanicville also provided access to southern gateways for freight carded in that direction. In the 1970s and 1980s most of Shaughnessy's photography was done with a Mamiya 67, a camera that afforded him more flexibility than his heavier 4 x 5. This is one such image made with the smaller camera.

Plate 139   New York Central local freight with RS3 #8278 and baggage cart, Tupper Lake, New York, August 1958

A local freight on New York Central's Adirondack Branch switches cars at the village of Tupper Lake with one of its considerable-sized fleet of Alco RS3 diesels, #8278. A baggage cart and country depot with REA signs frame the composition. The line was originally financed with the aid of New York Central capital supplied by physician turned railroad promoter Dr. William Seward Webb, William Vanderbilt's son-in-law. Initially named the Adirondack & St. Lawrence, it was built to tap the tourist potential of the mountain area and, secondarily, to reach Webb's deluxe "great camp" on the Fulton chain of lakes. The line was eventually absorbed by the New York Central in the 1890s and became the basis for its route not only through the heart of the Adirondack Mountains but on to Montreal as well.

Plate 140   Pennsylvania 2–10–0 and 100-car coal train along State Highway 14, Ralston, Pennsylvania, May 5, 1957

A massive 2–10–0, I-1-class PRR steam locomotive—one of 565 once rostered on the PRR—labors mightily with 100 cars of coal bound for Sodus Point, New York, on the Elmira Branch running between Williamsport, Pennsylvania, and the shore of Lake Ontario at a point east of Rochester, New York.

Plate 141   New York Central, *Laurentian* and observation car, Troy Union Station, Troy, New York, March 12, 1955

The Montreal-to-New York City day train the *Laurentian* is ready to depart Troy Union Station on NYC's line down the east side of the Hudson River. The NYC through observation/lounge car runs on the D&H's section in New York state along the west shore of Lake Champlain, while the Rutland's goes through Vermont on the east side of the lake. The two sections are combined in Troy for the final leg of the journey into the Big Apple. Troy Union Station, built in the Beaux Arts tradition, saw 120 passenger trains a day in 1914. By 1958 that number had dwindled to eight daily B&M trains—four in each direction. In this scene Shaughnessy is up in Tower #2, a unique piece of railroad architecture that guarded train movements into the station.

Plate 142   Two Nickel Plate workers and 2–8–4 Berkshire #731 and sister locomotive in roundhouse, Conneaut, Ohio, 1957

Two grease-covered workers walk past a lineup of Nickel Plate Road 2–8–4 Berkshires in the roundhouse at Conneaut, Ohio. The NKP —which ran from Chicago and St. Louis to Buffalo—relied on its fleet of steam locomotives long after other railroads had completely dieselized due primarily to the fact they had relatively new Super Power locomotives and meticulously maintained them.

Plate 143   Canadian Pacific double-headed steam locomotives and freight train, Lennoxville, Quebec, January 20, 1954

The –20°F morning air of Lennoxville, Quebec, is filled with the sight and sound of two smoke-belching Canadian Pacific steam locomotives approaching the St. Francis River bridge as they head east through the Eastern Townships of the La Belle Province with a heavy train of prairie grain bound for Saint John, New Brunswick. This image is one of the photographer's favorites.

Plate 143 Canadian Pacific double-headed steam locomotives and freight train, Lennoxville, Quebec, 1954

Notes

1. Susan Danly and Leo Marx, *The Railroad in American Art: Representations of Technological Change* (Cambridge, MA: MIT Press, 1988), 183.

2. Stewart Holbrook, *The Story of American Railroads* (New York: Bonanza Books, 1957), 1.

3. Danly and Marx, *The Railroad in American Art,* 52, 72

4. Henry David Thoreau, *Walden* (New York, Toronto: Rinehart & Company, 1956), 75.

5. Danly and Marx, *The Railroad in American Art,* 51.

6. "History of Troy, New York (As a Village)," http://history.rays place.com/ny/ren-troy-village-ny.htm.

7. Wikipedia, http://en.wikipedia.org/wiki/False-collar; "Labor and Industry in Troy and Cohoes: A Brief History," http://www.albany.edu/history/Troy-Cohoes/.

8. "History of Troy, New York, Part 1," http://www.trivia-library.com/b/history-of-troy-new-york-part-1.htm.

9. "Rensselaer Railroad Heritage," http://railroad.union.rpi.edu/article.php?article=822.

10. "Labor and Industry in Troy and Cohoes: A Brief History."

11. Interview with Jim Shaughnessy, Troy, New York, January 18, 2007.

12. http://www.whitehouse.gov/history/presidents/fr32.html.

13. Wikipedia, http://en.wikipedia.org/wiki/Troy,_New_York. Gurley's theodolites were used to survey much of the American West after the Civil War and were highly regarded until laser and digital technology eclipsed telescope and compass technology in the 1970s.

14. RensSearch, http://vcmr108.server.rpi.edu/archives/buildings/university_building.html.

15. Interview with Jim Shaughnessy, Troy, New York, January 18, 2007.

16. *Trains,* November 1955, 33.

17. Interview with Jim Shaughnessy, Troy, New York, January 18, 2007.

18. Between 1871 and 1920, 26.3 million people arrived in the United States as immigrants; see Douglas Rae, *City Urbanism and its End* (New Haven: Yale University Press, 2003), 15.

19. John Stilgoe, *Metropolitan Corridor* (New Haven: Yale University Press, 1983).

20. Interview with Jim Shaughnessy, Troy, New York, May 8, 2007.

21. E-mail correspondence with Jim Shaughnessy, January 8, 2007.

22. Phone interview with Greg McDonnell, Kitchener, Ontario, June 2007.

23. This language is borrowed from David P. Morgan talking about the work of Linn Wescott, *Trains,* March 1985, p. 36. It seems an apt description, based on Greg McDonnell's comments, of Worthen's sensibilities as well.

24. Interview with Jim Shaughnessy, Troy, New York, May 8, 2007.

25. Ibid.

26. Kodak Classics, http://kodak.3106.net/index.php?p=208&cam=1240.

27. Interview with Jim Shaughnessy, Troy, New York, July 7, 2007.

28. Ibid.

29. "I draw something from being in nature, but I don't use it. It bores. Those who do [use nature] like [Eliot] Porter and [Ansel] Adams bore me. I'm not interested in their art. I don't even call it art. I'm interested in the hand of man and civilization." Walker Evans, *The Hungry Eye* (New York: Abrams, 1993), 13.

30. The exhibition ran from October 18 to November 25, 1962.

31. John Raeburn, *A Staggering Revolution: A Cultural History of Thirties Photography* (Chicago: University of Illinois Press, 2006), states that the FSA's contemporary visibility is misleading. In fact, the photographs "never became more than irregular journalistic fare," with *Life* and *Look* only publishing a handful, often failing even to credit them (pp. 144–45). I'm also of the opinion that most railfans in the 1940s and 1950s using photography to record their favorite subject did not follow trends or movements pertaining to fine-art photog-

raphy or documentary photography of the era. For most railfans photography was a means to an end, not something to be thought about for its own aesthetic merits. Although Walker Evans did receive some notice for his "American Photographs" exhibition at MoMA in 1938, the audience in the United States at the time for "art" photography was small; photography wasn't even considered a respectable art form by most museums. The four railroad-themed portfolios Evans produced during his tenure at *Fortune* (1945–1965) had a definite impact on the work of David Plowden—a contemporary photographer and protégé of Evans's who also has an affinity for vernacular sujects. But in the main a magazine whose contents were geared toward white-collar financial advisers, stockbrokers, and corporate CEOs would have been a publication unlikely to be read by train buffs. Therefore Evans's influence within the blue-collar railfan photography community of the day would have been questionable. It should also be noted that, according to author John T. Hill, after Evans left *Fortune* in 1965 his work still had no popular appeal (Evans, *The Hungry Eye,* p. 304).

32. Phone interview with Jim Shaughnessy, September 24, 2007. Perhaps the images he saw were those made by Horace Bristol that appeared in *Life* in 1940.

33. February 1942 *Trains* images appear on pp. 9 and 15. For additional FSA or OWI (Office of War Information) photos that appeared in *Trains,* see the March 1942 issue with an article entitled *Rush—Perishable,* pp. 12–16. It contains for the most part standard-issue FSA fare (what Roy Stryker referred to as "record" shots), except for the grain elevator and boxcar image on p. 13, which became an icon of the era (and would fall into the FSA "art" category). Also see *Trains,* May 1943, 41, for a "photo by Hollem, Office of War Information."

34. In my estimation the early work of John Gruber suggests a Robert Frank influence, with its dark overtones, grainy 35mm film, and emotional resonance. See Jeff Brouws and Ed Delvers, *Starlight on the Rails* (New York: Abrams, 2000), 45, 127.

35. Smith's essay "A Man of Mercy: Africa's misery turns saintly Albert Schweitzer into a driving taskmaster," appeared in *Life,* November 15, 1954, 161–72; the Pittsburgh images, though commissioned in 1955 by

historian Stefan Lorant, did not appear in print at length until *Dream Street, W. Eugene Smith's Pittsburgh Project* was published in 2001 (*Dream Street, W. Eugene Smith's Pittsburgh Project,* Durham: Lyndhurst Books, 2001).

36. Interview with Jim Shaughnessy, Troy, New York, January 18, 2007.

37. Wally Abbey was a former newspaper photographer from Kansas City, a member of *Trains*'s staff from 1950–54, and a journalism student at Kansas University shooting trains around Chicago in 1942. See *Trains,* November 1955, 36. Richard Steinheimer studied under Joe Rosenthal at San Francisco City College in 1949–50.

38. According to Thomas Garver, Link didn't recall seeing major film noir movies from the era such as *The Third Man* or *Touch of Evil.* Nonetheless Garver suggests Link's N&W nighttime pictures share a similar cinematic and theatrical sensibility. O. Winston Link, *The Last Steam Railroad in America* (New York: Abrams, 1995), 23.

39. The article "What Is a Freight Train?" was a sweeping panoramic view of the intersection of railroading and American culture. *Trains,* September 1953, 38–57.

40. See *Trains,* February 1950, 47-49; *Trains,* November 1955, 31–45; *Trains,* March 1957, 30–45.

41. The Precisionist artist Charles Sheeler made images that contained some railroad material inside Ford's River Rouge plant in 1927. He also made a key modernist photograph of locomotive driving wheels in 1939 (*Power Series, Wheels*). Lewis Hine, a well-known documentary photographer, also shot in rail yards making portraits of workers on the Pennsylvania Railroad in the 1920s. However, neither artist would be considered a railfan photographer.

42. In my opinion, after looking at Shaughnessy's entire archive, he undoubtedly shot more rail images at night than any other known twentieth-century photographer. In fact, almost 10 percent of his entire output was dedicated to after-dark imagery, all made on 4 x 5 sheet film. See *Night Train* (San Marino: Pacific Railway Journal, 1961) for an excellent overview of this body of work.

43. S. Berliner III, Champlain College, http://home.attnet/~Berliner-Ultrasonics/champcol.html.

44. Interview with Jim Shaughnessy Troy, New York, January 18, 2007.

45. Ibid.

46. Quote attributed to Hastings while on a trip one year earlier with David Morgan, shooting the same line. See *Mohawk That Refused to Abdicate* (Milwaukee: Kalmbach Publishing Co., 1975), 199.

47. Information gleaned from Shaughnessy's timekeeping books and various interviews with Shaughnessy conducted in 2007.

48. Ibid.

49. "Focal Power" (blog), http://blog.focal power.com/2007/07/13/remembering-john-szarkowski-in-his-own-words/.

50. Interview with Jim Shaughnessy, Troy, New York, July 7, 2007.

51. Ibid.

52. Ibid.

53. Lee Friedlander, "An Excess of Fact," *The Desert Seen* (New York: D.A.P, 1996), 103.

54. Tony Reevy, "Jim Shaughnessy: Artist of the Rail," *NRHS Bulletin*, Spring 2007, 12.

55. *New York Times,* News and Features, http://nymag.com/nymetro/news/yearinreview/2004/10664/.

56. Gadget video clips, http://www.gadgetvids .com/view/27909.

57. Lecture given by Rudy Vanderlans at the Pacific Design Center, Los Angeles, California, spring 1994.

58. Interview with Jim Shaughnessy, Troy, New York, May 8, 2007.

59. The rare occasions where Shaughnessy deviated from this were the Rutland trestle photos. This had more to do with varying camera angles to take maximum advantage of the flashbulbs and lighting than multiple frames of the same setup (it was also one of the few times he deployed a large group of friends to aid him with the photography; multiple cameras were used as well).

60. Shaughnessy stood next to Baxter and made an image at the same time. See Jim Shaughnessy, *The Rutland Road* (Berkeley, CA: Howell-North Books, 1964), 326.

61. Douglas M. Nelson, *Philip R. Hastings, Portrait of the Pennsylvania Railroad* (Los Angeles: Pine Tree Press, 2002), 125.

62. James Elkins, *Visual Studies: A Skeptical Introduction* (New York and London: Routledge, 2003), 4. Roeder, "Filling in the Picture: Visual Culture," *Reviews in American History* 26:1 (1998): 275–93, quotation on p. 275.

63. Walker Evans, "When Downtown Was a Beautiful Mess," *Fortune*, January 1962, 101.

64. Photographs by George Barnard (1819–1902) on Library of Congress American Memoryloc.gov/cgibin/query/D?cwar:4:./temp/~ammem_Eara.

65. *Encyclopedia Britannica*, http://www.britannica.com/eb/article-252867/photo graphy-history of#416456.hook.

66. Interview with Jim Shaughnessy, Troy, New York, December 2006.

67. Ibid.

68. Interview with Jim Shaughnessy, Troy, New York, May 8, 2007.

69. Lucius Beebe and Charles Clegg, *Rio Grande, Mainline of The Rockies* (Berkeley, CA: Howell-North Books, 1962), 360–61.

70. Interview with Jim Shaughnessy, Troy, New York, December 2006.

71. E-mail correspondence with Jim Boyd, May 18, 2007.

72. Interview with Jim Shaughnessy, Troy, New York, May 8, 2007.

73. Ibid. Though Shaughnessy handled the flash duties when traveling with Phil Hastings, it's apparent from the printed record that Hastings was using open flash for night pictures before 1956. Jim states on p. 124 of *Philip R. Hastings, Portrait of the Pennsylvania Railroad* that he had "introduced him [Hast-ings] to open flash lighting of scenes that would otherwise be totally dark" during the Brattleboro CV roundhouse shoot in April 1956. Apparently Shaughnessy was either unfamiliar with Hastings's earlier work or assumed (because Phil deferred, letting Jim fire the flashes) that Hastings was unfamiliar with the technique—an easy mistake to make. In any event, Hastings was already adept at open flash as his image in *Starlight on the Rails* (p. 112), made in 1953, attests.

74. It appears some of Philip Hastings's first published night photographs using open flash and time exposure appeared in *Trains*, July 1950, 42, and September 1950, 25.

75. Pacing shots as seen in *Trains* June 1950, 32, by A. C. Kalmbach; March 1953, 45, by David Conner; November 1951, 28, by F. Le Jaques.

76. Shaughnessy shot four rolls of 2¼ film for a day-in-the-life feature on D&H hostler Henry Stewart, who worked at its Whitehall, New York, yard, in June 1957; writer Rob Craib accompanied him.

77. Lucius Beebe and Charles Clegg books in which Shaughnessy photographs can be found are:
Great Railroad Photographs, USA (Berkeley, CA: Howell-North Books, 1964); *When Beauty Rode the Rails* (Garden City, NY: Doubleday & Co., 1962); *The Central Pacific and Southern Pacific Railroads* (Berkeley, CA: Howell-North Books, 1963); *Rio Grande: Mainline of the Rockies* (Berkeley, CA: Howell-North Books, 1962); *Narrow Gauge on the Rio Grande* (Berkeley, CA: Howell-North Books, 1958); *The Age of Steam* (New York: Rinehart Publications, 1957); *The Trains We Rode Vol I* (Berkeley, CA: Howell-North Books, 1965); *The Trains We Rode Vol II* (Berkeley, CA: Howell-North Books, 1966).

78. Interview with Jim Shaughnessy, Troy, New York, May 8, 2007.

79. *Railfan* magazine, March 2005, review of *A Passion for Trains*, p. 14.

80. Shaughnessy, *The Rutland Road* , 129.

81. Ibid.

82. Richard Saunders Jr. *Merging Lines* (DeKalb: Northern Illinois University Press, 2001), 7–8.

83. Shaughnessy, *The Rutland Road*, 147. The Rutland went into receivership on May 5, 1938.

84. Ibid., 129.

85. Abandonment or merger dates for the various railroads were: NYC, 1968; B&M (bankruptcy in 1970, reorganization by Guilford Industries in 1983); RUT, 1963; NYO&W, 1957.

86. Saunders, *Merging Lines*, 100.

87. Shaughnessy, *The Rutland Road*, 129.

88. Saunders, *Merging Lines*, 103.

89. L. Leslie Waters, *Railroads from World War II to Date and Beyond* (Bloomington, 1975), Graduate School of Business, Indiana University, 143, available at: http://www.hnet.org/~business/bhcweb /publications/BEHprint/v004/p0137-p0151.pdf.

90. Interview with Jim Shaughnessy, Troy, New York, May 8, 2007.

91. When Jim handed me the shoe box containing approximately 300 D&H neg-atives of Sharks and PAs he said: "Here's the good stuff." As most of these were builder-type photos taken around the exterior or inside of the Colonie shops, I immediately understood that he was very fond of what the images contained and wasn't commenting necessarily about their value as art but on their value as historical documents.

92. For a discussion of the shift from black and white to color in railfan photography, see Jeff Brouws, *A Passion for Trains, The Railroad Photography of Richard Steinheimer* (New York: W. W. Norton, 2004), 28.

93. Talk with Arthur Ollman; quote attributed to John Szarkowski, Carpinteria, California, March 1992.

94. For additional biographical material on Shaughnessy, see Tony Reevy, "Jim Shaughnessy: Artist of the Rail," *NRHS Bulletin*, Spring 2007, 4–23.

Acknowledgments

Acknowledgments for Jim Shaughnessy

Two individuals deserve huge credit for prompting me into action on this project: Jeff Brouws and his wife, Wendy. His expertise in the field of art photography and previous offerings of this type and her long association with the publishing industry have resulted in the volume before you.

Others have also influenced the creation of this volume in varying degrees and ways. The late David P. Morgan, longtime editor of *Trains*, accepted my work and featured it on the pages of that magazine. The late Lucius Beebe, considered by many, including me, to be the father of the railroad book as we know it today, sought out my photos and featured them in many of his wonderful books. The late Morgan North, of Howell–North Books, accepted my manuscripts and photos and with them the production of two books: *The Rutland Road* and *Delaware and Hudson*. Publisher Donald Duke accepted my suggestion and used 80 percent of my work in the first all-night photo book of trains, *Night Train*. John Gruber of the Center for Railroad Photography and Art has penned kind words about my work and featured it in several expositions.

My parents, James and Helen Shaughnessy, were needless to say there from the beginning and in my adolescent years gave me the opportunity to travel, see, experience, and photograph many railroad situations that would develop into an even greater dimension as years passed. My uncle Cornelius (Con), who once worked for the D&H as a valvesetter on steam locomotives, inoculated me with an interest in railroads and its equipment as a diversion during some business trips I took with him as a safety engineer for the Hartford Insurance Company. The late Rev. Raymond J. Halpin introduced me to darkroom procedures and was an early traveling companion. Also, John Pickett and the late Sanborn S. (Sandy) Worthen provided fine company on numerous journeys.

Finally, I want to acknowledge the folks at Kalmbach Publishing—Kevin Keefe, Dave Ingles, Rob McGonigal, Jim Wrinn, and Greg McDonnell—and those at Carstens Publishing—Jim Boyd, Steve Barry, and Walter Lankenau—for their past and continuing offering of my work.

To you all, living and dead—I thank you!

Acknowledgments for Jeff Brouws

Books need to have reasons for coming into existence, and I can think of no better than a desire to see (between covers) a culminating visual statement about one photographer's life's work. I thank Jim Shaughnessy for giving us the opportunity to make this presentation of his railroad imagery: if he hadn't worked so tirelessly and thoroughly during the final hours of steam railroading in America and Canada, we and the historical record would be that much poorer and this book wouldn't exist. His dedication deserves our attention. I also appreciate Jim's generosity and intellectual curiosity: he answered arcane questions and endured multiple interviews as we ferreted out the facts of his life and photographic pursuits. I think we both enjoyed this process; his patience over the past two years is much appreciated.

While assembling the myriad components of this project, many friends, publishing colleagues, and family members offered crucial assistance and advice. I want to acknowledge and thank everyone for this support. I'd like first and foremost to give kudos to my wife, Wendy Burton Brouws, who not only was responsible for our interface with W. W. Norton, acting as she did as book agent, but also lent the defining hand in shaping *The Call of Trains: Railroad Photographs by Jim Shaughnessy*. Her expert sequencing and visual editing skills are in evidence throughout; she came up with the title too. Thanks also to our editor, editorial assistant and marketing specialist at W. W. Norton: Jim Mairs, Austin O'Driscoll, and Bill Rusin, who lent their own brands of skill, energy, and enthusiasm to these pages. Dear friend John Pickett offered invaluable firsthand accounts of traveling with Jim Shaughnessy during the 1950s and 1960s; the essay is richer for his contribution. Philip Dossick, Robert Mohowski, and Karl Zimmerman read my manuscript at various stages and offered insightful commentary on how it might be improved. Lastly, the work of fellow artists and scholars (or their presence in our memories and hearts) continues to provide valuable sparks of inspiration: Shirley Burman, Carson Burrington, Nell Campbell, Kathryn Clark, Sally Culpeck, Ed Delvers, Wayne Depperman, "E-Train" Edelstein, John Gerlitz, John Gruber, Ron Hill, Joel Jensen, Simpson Kalisher, Greg McDonnell, Robert Mohowski, Barb Parmet, Mel Patrick, David Plowden, Chad Smith, Richard Steinheimer, Karl Zimmerman, and our friends at the Center for Railroad Photography and Art in Madison, Wisconsin.

The Call of Trains: Railroad Photographs by Jim Shaughnessy

Photographs copyright © 2008 by Jim Shaughnessy

"Railroading Landscapes: The Photography of Jim Shaughnessy" copyright © 2008 by Jeff Brouws

Caption text copyright © 2008 by Jim Shaughnessy and Jeff Brouws

"Looking Back: Sixty Years of Railroad Photography" copyright © 2008 by Jim Shaughnessy

All rights reserved
Printed in Italy
First Edition

Manufactured by Mondadori Publishing Inc.
Special thanks to Sergio Brunelli and Nancy Freeman

Design: Jeff Brouws, For A Small Fee, Inc.
Image sequencing: Wendy Burton Brouws

Library of Congress Cataloging-in-Publication Data
Shaughnessy, Jim.
   The call of trains : railroad photographs by Jim Shaughnessy / Text by Jeff Brouws.
      p. cm.
   ISBN 978-0-393-06592-3 (hardcover)
   1. Photography of railroads. 2. Railroads--United States--Pictorial works. I. Brouws, Jeff. II. Title.
   TR715.S43 2008
   779'.9385--dc22

                                    2008001295

W. W. Norton & Company, Inc.
500 Fifth Avenue, New York, New York 10110
www.wwnorton.com

W. W. Norton & Company, Ltd.
Castle House, 75/76 Wells Street, London, WIT 3QT

1 2 3 4 5 6 7 8 9 0

Exhibition schedule:

The Call of Trains:
Railroad Photographs by Jim Shaughnessy
California State Railroad Museum,
January 23, 2009–July 2009